LEARNING to PRAY

LEARNING *to* PRAY

DISCOVERING
THE HEART OF GOD

DEBORAH KERN

© 2009 by Deborah J. Kern. All rights reserved.
2nd Printing 2014

No part of this publication may be reproduced, stored in a retrieval system, or transmitted in any way by any means—electronic, mechanical, photocopy, recording, or otherwise—without the prior permission of the copyright holder, except as provided by USA copyright law.

Unless otherwise noted, all Scriptures are taken from the *Holy Bible, New International Version*, NIV*. Copyright © 1973, 1978, 1984 by the International Bible Society. Used by permission of Zondervan. All rights reserved.

Scripture references marked KJV are taken from the *King James Version* of the Bible.

Scripture references marked NASB are taken from the *New American Standard Bible,* © 1960, 1963, 1968, 1971, 1972, 1973, 1975, 1977 by The Lockman Foundation. Used by permission.

Scripture references marked NKJV are taken from the New King James Version. Copyright © 1982 by Thomas Nelson, Inc. Used by permission. All rights reserved.

Scripture quotations marked "TLB" or "The Living Bible" are taken from The Living Bible [computer file] / Kenneth N. Taylor.—electronic ed.—Wheaton : Tyndale House, 1997, c1971 by Tyndale House Publishers, Inc. Used by permission. All rights reserved.

Scripture quotations are taken from *THE MESSAGE*, copyright © 1993, 1994, 1995, 1996, 2000, 2001, 2002. Used by permission of NavPress Publishing Group.

Library of Congress Catalog Card Number: 2008904636

Contents

Coming to God
1. Prayer Is for You 1
2. Intimate Friends 7
3. The Fervent Pursuit 15
4. A New Control 21
5. Help 29
6. Getting Started 41

Learning from God
7. Face to Face with God 51
8. Why We Wait 59
9. When God Says No 67
10. Cleaning Time 75
11. Repentance: Grief and Joy 85
12. Trading Rocks for Jewels 95
13. What Does God Sound Like? 103
14. When We Wander 111

Walking with God
15. What God Really Wants 121
16. The Beauty of the Ordinary 129
17. Should I Pray About It? 137
18. God's Call 145

19. Trusting 153
20. Struggling in the Stillness 161
21. Growing Closer 171

Working with God
22. Not Just My Own Needs 181
23. Don't Stop Now 191
24. New Strength for Prayer 199
25. Armed and Ready 209
26. Untangling Lives 221
27. Reaching for True Faith 231
28. In His Time and Season 241
29. Will You Come? 249

Coming to God

Come to me,
all you who are weary and burdened,
and I will give you rest.
—Matthew 11:28

CHAPTER 1

Prayer Is for You

My daughter, Jula, started piano lessons when she was seven. She had begun to try to learn on her own, and I realized it was time to give her some formal lessons. I put her in a group class and watched to see how she did. In only a few weeks I realized I had a musical genius on my hands. Instead of practicing the required half hour a day, she spent at least an hour at the piano. She learned every song in her first book in a month and advanced to the next class, where she quickly caught up and soon surpassed their level.

I was thrilled. With this kind of drive and talent there was no limit to what she could accomplish! Sometimes I would stand just outside the door listening to "The Wigwam Song," "Go Tell Aunt Rhody," or "Little Swiss Clock," while in my mind I heard the distant strains of Chopin and Bach. I could almost see Carnegie Hall—the crowded audiences, the standing ovations…

But summer came along and the teacher gave the students a month of vacation. Soon I realized that I hadn't heard Jula play the piano in days. Oh, well, I thought, everyone needs a break. When lessons began again, I was sure she would be back at it.

However, fall came and the lessons resumed, but the practicing did not. Just like every other mother trying to force a cultural activity into her child's life, I began to have to make Jula practice.

After a while I sadly began to realize that perhaps Carnegie Hall might not be in Jula's future. However, I was not willing to let her give up completely. After a few weeks of nagging her to practice, I decided the key was to motivate her in some way. She obviously just needed help getting back in the groove after her vacation.

About that time, Jula's teacher gave her the music for "Tomorrow" from the movie *Annie*. It was much harder than anything she had ever done, but she had only been asked to learn the melody line of the first page.

I knew how much Jula loved that song. I also knew what else she loved—ice cream! So I went in one day while she was practicing and sat on the piano bench next to her.

"Jula, if you really worked on this piece like you did the songs last spring, you could learn all of it, not just the right hand. And I'll tell you what—if you can learn it all, both right and left hands, all the way through in two weeks, I'll buy you the biggest ice cream sundae you've ever seen."

Nothing thrills Jula like ice cream, so I glanced over to see her delight. But instead, I watched her face crumple and her lip begin to quiver. Soon she was crying heartbroken, disappointed tears.

I was amazed. "What's wrong?"

"I can't do it!" She sat there with her arms folded tight against her chest and looked up at me with hurt, accusing eyes.

I tried to talk to her about it, but I soon realized she was convinced it was impossible for her. She absolutely didn't believe she could do it.

That hadn't been important...until I dangled ice cream in front of her. Now it mattered. She was going to lose out on the biggest ice cream sundae she had ever seen.

An ice cream sundae was great, but if she couldn't reach the goal, why even mention it? Instead of motivating Jula, all I had done was frustrate her.

I thought of this incident the other day when I asked a friend what she thought about a prayer seminar we had both attended.

"I just couldn't relate to it." She shook her head in frustration as she told me it was too far over her head.

Sometimes it's that way for us, too. We hear about the positive victories that other people experience in prayer. We hear about the dedication, the discipline, and the rewards, but instead of motivating us, these things sometimes end up discouraging us.

Speakers on prayer and authors of books about prayer often seem to forget what it's like for the average Christian who has not developed the same prayer life they have. They relate incredible stories about answers to prayer, talk about praying for hours, and casually mention they fast a day a week. Then they go on to tell us that we hold the key to making a difference in the world, whether it's for a loved one's salvation or world evangelism. Some people feel exhilarated at the thought, but others experience an overwhelming sense of responsibility and even despair. Just like Jula, they don't feel motivated—they feel frustrated and defeated.

Perhaps you've felt that way when you have heard people sharing about their victories in prayer. Perhaps you have set out to be more consistent in your prayer life in the past, but always seemed to fail. Perhaps you've heard yourself saying things such as:

"I'm not disciplined enough."
"I don't have time."
"I don't have enough faith."
"It doesn't seem to do much good."

I have good news for you. Prayer is not just for the speakers at prayer seminars or the authors of prayer manuals. It's not just for the motivated and self-disciplined, and it is not just for the intercessory prayer warriors or people in ministry.

Prayer is for you, and God created prayer so that everyone could come to Him and sit at His feet. He wants it to be more than the

"pray when I'm in trouble"
"pray on Sunday"
"pray when I'm feeling spiritual"

hit-and-miss prayer life that so many Christians seem to have.

God created prayer in such a way that a consistent, life-changing prayer life would not be out of anyone's reach. In failing to pray consistently, perhaps you have also failed to grasp the significance, the importance, the all-encompassing reality of your relationship with God. It is eternal. It has the might and purpose of the almighty Creator of the universe behind it, and prayer is part of His overall plan of developing a relationship with you.

God wants you to pray. He has not failed to do all that is necessary to establish a relationship with you, beginning with the creation of the world, continuing through the death and resurrection of His Son, Jesus, and His personal work in drawing you to salvation. He will also help you to pray!

Developing a consistent, effective prayer life doesn't happen overnight, however. There are lessons to be learned about prayer, steps to be taken in learning to pray consistently and effectively, and most important, a relationship to be built with an all-powerful yet intimate and loving God.

Wherever you are in your prayer life—whether you are just starting out, whether you are still just trying to be consistent, or whether you've been praying for years, there is something here for you because this book is about your relationship with God as revealed by your prayer life. It can help you develop a pattern of growth in prayer that, at the same time, brings growth to your personal relationship with God.

Learning what prayer is all about and endeavoring to be consistent is the first step involved in learning to pray. From that point, you will discover how God wants to use your prayer life as a time of interaction so that you come to know Him and His ways.

As you begin to know God, you will gradually want to involve Him in more areas of your life. When this happens, your life becomes one that, more and more, is shared fully with God.

As you continue to forge ahead in your prayer relationship, you'll find that as you become more intimately involved with God, you will begin to take on His concerns and desires. You will increasingly want to see His will done on earth, and your heart will be stirred to pray for others in intercession.

Soon your relationship with God will have deepened, and your heart will be intertwined with His in a way you would never have dreamed possible.

In the beginning, however, many of our initial conversations with God will revolve around our needs. That's okay. God created prayer as a means of receiving His assistance, so it is never wrong to come to Him with our needs and desires. That is what He wants us to do.

> Come to me, all you who are weary and burdened, and I will give you rest. Take my yoke upon you and learn from me, for I am gentle and humble in heart, and you will find rest for your souls.
> —Matthew 11:28-29

Reflect

If you have started reading this book, it means that you are interested in prayer and have a desire for growth in this area of your life.

How would you describe your prayer life?

_____

_____

Does coming to God bring "rest" into your life? _____

How would you describe your relationship with God the Father and His son, Jesus?

_____

Along with your desire for growth in your prayer life, is there also a desire to know God better?

_____

Whatever the state of your relationship with God, I know you will agree there is room for growth. Very few of us have as intimate and personal a relationship with God as we would like.

Think about what you desire in the area of relationship with God and then write it down in the space given.

_____

Receiving God's Invitation

Look up Matthew 11:28-29 in your Bible.

Underline it and write your name after the word "Me." Take out the word "all" and read it again with your own name inserted. Think of this verse as God's personal invitation to you today. Using your prayer diary or the space below, write out a responsive prayer.

Discussion

What areas do you find easy to pray about now, if any?

In what areas of your life would you like to involve God more?

What is your greatest problem with prayer?

Share some of your answers to the questions in the "reflect" section, specifically: Does coming to God bring "rest" into your life?

CHAPTER 2

Intimate Friends

It was time for a vacation, and this time I had it all under control. The morning we were to leave I was up early getting everything organized. I barked out orders, rushing everyone around, reminding them of what still needed to be done. I kept everyone's nose to the grindstone, checking off my list as items were placed in the car. Yes, I really had it all together.

We had everything we needed for a wonderful time. There were snacks for the kids and games to play in the car so I wouldn't have to listen to "Mama, Jula's on my side" or "Matt touched me!"

I had the maps, the itinerary, the sunglasses, and the coffee thermos. And this time I had even thought ahead and brought some teaching tapes to listen to while we were traveling.

We started out, and I sat there feeling pleased with myself. I hadn't forgotten a thing. After about an hour I put one of the tapes in and started it up. It was on parenting and had some excellent thoughts on communication and family meetings. However, it wasn't long before I was straining to hear it. The kids sure were being noisy.

I turned the volume up, but the noise level increased all the more as they shouted to be heard above it. I turned around and told them to be quiet and then reached over to turn up the volume again. When Jula yelled a question at me I snapped back in exasperation, quickly stabbing at buttons in order to go back and hear what I had missed. Then Chuck, my husband, asked me a question, and I answered him curtly, starting the tape once again as I rolled my eyes in annoyance at all the interruptions.

Finally I reached over in frustration and snapped the cassette player off, turning to glare at those responsible for my predicament. Then I sat there feeling sorry for myself.

As the noise level subsided and the car became unnaturally silent, I suddenly realized what I was doing. I was trying to listen to a tape on effective parenting...when I should be parenting! And all that morning I had been busily arranging everybody and everything for a family trip so we could be together and make family memories. Yet my heavy-handed tactics had made everyone miserable.

I had become caught up in trying to take care of the mechanics of a good family life—even down to listening to a tape on parenting skills so I could do it right—and all the while I had a husband and two children who needed my love and my attention and my involvement in their lives right then.

We tend to do that with prayer, too. We get caught up in the mechanics and forget all about the basic reason for prayer.

Did you ever wonder why God asks us to pray? The Bible is full of statements encouraging us to pray and promises that God will hear and answer. But what is the purpose for prayer? Is it just a way to get God's attention and receive help when we need it?

John Wesley, the great eighteenth-century English church leader, once said, "God does nothing but in answer to prayer."

That is a pretty big statement. Why would God tie Himself to our prayers? Doesn't that limit Him?

One writer explained the reason for prayer as a kind of "overriding law of the universe" which enables God to be sovereign even while giving man free will. Prayer permits God to exercise His sovereignty in a world under the domination of people with free will, in a universe governed by natural law.

He is saying *as you and I pray, we are asking for God's will to be done in the world, and that releases God to intervene and accomplish His good.* Interesting thought.

In our question of "why pray" it is important to remember that God does not "need" prayer. God, who is all powerful, sovereign, and complete in everything, does not "need" anything to be able to act in accordance with His divine character and purposes. It does seem however, in looking at the vast amount of scriptures telling us to "ask and I will answer," that God "requires" prayer as a prerequisite to His intervention in the world.

So is that it? Is prayer simply a method to enable God to intervene in the world, necessary because of His sovereignty and our free will?

There's a familiar story in Genesis about God coming to see Abraham. He came in the form of a man along with two angels. Abraham immediately brought them into his home, made them comfortable, and prepared a lavish meal for them.

You may have heard the story many times: God had come to tell Abraham and Sarah that they were about to have a son, even though Sarah was too old to conceive. It's fun to picture the expression on Sarah's face when God read her doubting thoughts and repeated them to her.

And then, if we keep reading through the second part of the story where God reveals to Abraham that He intends to destroy Sodom and Gomorrah, we see the first example in the Bible of intercession. Abraham bargained with God to prevent Him from destroying the city because his nephew, Lot, lived there. However, it is the introduction to the second part of this narrative that reveals the real reason God came in the way He did.

After eating dinner, when the men got up to leave, Abraham walked along with them on their way. The Lord said to His companions, "Shall I hide from Abraham what I am about to do?"

The beauty of the story for me lies not in the fact that God gave Abraham the opportunity to intercede, although it is an important principle, but in the very act of God telling Abraham about His plans.

"Shall I hide from Abraham what I am about to do?"

This reveals so much to us about the nature of God and His desire for intimacy and fellowship with mankind.

Remember that God created human beings in order to have fellowship with them. He had come daily to the garden to be with Adam and Eve until sin intervened, causing a barrier between God and man. There had been no recorded incident of humans coming into intimate contact with God since the days of Enoch and Noah. But now, God had come to talk to Abraham.

Was it just to allow Abraham to intercede? Is that the whole lesson for us here?

Learning to Pray

Before Christ came to provide a way into God's presence for every man, the people who were able to enjoy fellowship with God were few and far between—Abraham, Jacob, Moses, some of the judges, Samuel, David, the prophets—yet each one we read about further reveals the aspect of God that wants to be involved with man: His willingness to visit Abraham; His night of wrestling with Jacob; allowing Moses to see His glory; coming in the night to call Samuel.

Constantly we see God moving toward mankind, giving people the opportunity to respond—to come and meet with Him in a one-on-one encounter.

God's visit with Abraham wasn't just to allow him to intercede. God's intent was to be with Abraham.

God desires to be known by us: to show us what He is thinking and feeling, and sometimes, what He is planning. He wants to give us a glimpse into His very self.

God came in the form of a man to visit Abraham and Sarah, to tell them about the birth of their son. He could have sent an angel, but He came Himself. Then He prolonged His visit by discussing with Abraham His plans for Sodom and Gomorrah.

This was the omnipotent, all-knowing Creator of the universe taking the time to be with Abraham and discuss with him some upcoming events. He didn't have to do this. He wanted to do it.

God had not come to earth to talk to man since Adam and Eve. Now He was here to talk to Abraham.

God is always moving toward man. He continues to make the first step toward regaining the relationship for which He created mankind. But there must be a move on our part in order for that relationship to be established. We accept Christ. We reach out to receive God and the relationship begins, but, as in earthly relationships, there must be more in order for there to be any kind of real intimacy, any real knowing.

The initial opening of our heart and life to Jesus at salvation is only the beginning. When God created prayer as a way to allow His intervention in our world, it wasn't just to accomplish His will on earth, and it wasn't just to give us a way to get Him to act in our behalf. God tied Himself to prayer so He could be joined with mankind in ongoing communication that would enable the growth of intimacy.

Yes, He wants His will to be done in the earth. He wants to bring salvation to those who have not yet heard. He wants to reclaim the souls Satan has ensnared. He wants to set the captives free and bring His good into the world. But all the mighty works of salvation, restoration, healing, and deliverance He wants to accomplish in the world and in you begin and end in the simple desire for an intimate relationship with mankind, with you.

We fathom so little about God's great desire for us. The overwhelming intensity of it cannot be comprehended with our finite minds. God's desire for a relationship with you is behind all that has happened in the history of the world. It is also the catalyst behind the events of your personal life.

All is designed—from creation to the birth and death of Christ, through the history of the world and the spread of the gospel, down to your individual history—to enable God to draw you into a personal, intimate relationship with Him.

God designed the world and created mankind, and when sin entered the world, He sent His Son to redeem us so that He could have a relationship with us. He will not fail to personalize His work in order to accomplish His desire to know and be known by you.

Prayer is relationship with God. We can look at prayer with reluctance or enthusiasm, with fervor or apathy, with understanding or misgivings, with delight or dread—but until we pray, we do not know God.

Prayer is opening ourselves to God and asking Him to be a part of our lives, and it is becoming a part of His life. God wants you to know His love. He wants you to come to know His attributes and be drawn into a closer relationship with Him so there will be a sharing, an intimacy, and a bonding that enables Him to reveal Himself to you, and you to open yourself to Him.

However, that intimacy will never happen if you do not come to God. And it will not happen if prayer is only a duty to be performed, a method to receive God's help, or a tool to be used to gain God's intervention in the world.

Prayer must become much more than that to each of us. It must be more than a way to get something from God; it must become an encounter with God and something we do in order to be with God.

> The Lord is good to those whose hope is in him, to the one who seeks him.
> —Lamentations 3:25

Reflect

"The whole Bible is about the loneliness of God."
—G.K. Chesterton

Read Gen. 3:8-9

God, in His omniscience, knew where Adam and Eve were, yet He asked, "Where are you?"

Think about God's purpose for creating mankind—relationship. Reflect on the above quote. Then read the scripture again. Allow the question to take on a deep personal meaning for you.

Study

Why did Jesus come to make the name of God known? (John 17:26)

_____

_____

Why does God knock at the door of our heart? (Rev. 3:20)

_____

_____

Intimate Friends

What is God's ultimate goal? (Acts 17:26-27; Rev. 21:3)

_____

_____

Receiving God

God's desire for an intimate relationship with mankind could only be realized by making it possible for His Son, Jesus Christ, to live inside each one of us. We, then, can be included in the relationship Jesus has with the Father.

Have you taken the first step toward intimacy with God by accepting His Son, Jesus, into your life?

If not, you may do so today by praying this prayer:

> Dear Heavenly Father,
>
> I accept the gift of Your Son, Jesus Christ, and I receive Him into my life today. I believe and accept His virgin birth, His death on the cross, and His resurrection from the dead as Your plan to enable me to have a relationship with You.
>
> Please forgive me for my sins and make me part of Your forever family.
>
> I give my life to You today.
>
> Amen.

Receiving God's Call to Intimacy

God is a Person and can be known in increasing degrees of intimacy as we prepare our hearts for the wonder of it.
—A.W. Tozer (The Pursuit of God)

Prayer of Response

Dear Heavenly Father,

I want to learn to pray and I want to learn to know You better. I ask You to teach me to pray. Create in me a spiritual hunger and enlarge my capacity for You and for prayer. I submit myself to You. Help me to respond to Your call to come.

Amen.

Discussion

Is the concept of prayer as a way to establish and build your relationship with God a new thought to you?

If so, does it change your attitude about prayer?

CHAPTER 3

The Fervent Pursuit

Our prayer life is a good gauge of where we are in our willingness to have a relationship with God. Most of us seem to suffer from the dual emotions of wanting a better prayer life, but feeling we do not have the time, energy, or motivation to do anything about it. Once we understand God's purpose for prayer, the second step for many of us in developing a relationship with God is to come to terms with where our heart really is concerning prayer. We may have to acknowledge the fact that we're not sure we want an intimate relationship with God. We're not sure we want to encounter Him very often. The children of Israel had the same problem:

> When the people saw the thunder and lightning and heard the trumpet and saw the mountain in smoke, they trembled with fear. They stayed at a distance and said to Moses, "Speak to us yourself and we will listen. But do not have God speak to us or we will die."
> —Exodus 20:18-19

Their God, Yahweh, had revealed Himself to the children of Israel through signs and wonders—freeing them from slavery, delivering them from the Egyptians, parting the Red Sea, providing water from a rock, and giving them supernatural food to eat. Then He literally began to talk out loud to them from a mountain on fire.

It was simply too much for them. They couldn't handle it. They were used to living farther apart from God. The gods of Egypt were idols, and they certainly never spoke.

Now this! They were frightened! They liked the idea of God delivering them. They liked it when He took care of them, and they were ready to agree to the rules He was handing down if He would continue to watch over them.

They were willing to be His people, but they were not ready to hear His voice. They were not ready for that kind of intimacy, that kind of knowledge of God. They had the same problem many of us do. We want a relationship with God—we want His forgiveness, His power, and His help in our lives—but beyond that we tend to hold back. We deal with God through our pastor, our church, our Bible study leader, our Christian TV programs, saying in essence, "Speak to me through them, God," because, like the children of Israel, the thought of being face-to-face with God frightens us.

Why is this? First, we don't really know God yet. The children of Israel had much to learn about God. His nature, His character, and His great love for them were still beyond their understanding. The Israelites knew of the God of their fathers Abraham, Isaac, and Jacob, but all that was a long time ago and far removed from them. Their present history with God was still very short.

Not knowing God kept the Israelites from wanting to know Him, just as our lack of knowledge and understanding of God, our misconceptions, and our lack of interaction with Him keep us a little wary of too much intimacy.

Second, we hold back in our desire for an intimate relationship with God because we intuitively know that closeness to God, hearing His voice, and knowing Him in greater measure will mean coming further into the light of His presence. That light will begin to reflect on us, and down deep we're not sure we want that! Our insecurity makes us afraid of exposure. We can't believe God will like what He sees, and we're sure we won't like it either. We just don't want to take a chance. We haven't really experienced God's perfect and accepting love for us in personal interactions with Him, so it isn't real to us.

One day when our son Matthew was around five years old, I put him down for his nap. He was typical of most children; even though he needed a nap, he never wanted to stop playing and take one. But that day I put him in bed and firmly told him not to get back up. It was a Sunday afternoon, so I said that Daddy and I would be across the hall in our room taking a nap too.

We went in and lay down to rest. Pretty soon we heard some movement and looked up in time to see Matt sneaking past our room. He had his eyes shut, with one hand over them, as he moved quietly by our open door. A moment later we heard a thump. He had run into a wall.

We still laugh about the incident, remembering with a smile his childish reasoning. He simply thought if he couldn't see us, then we couldn't see him.

You and I think that way about God too—if we don't see Him too clearly, He probably isn't seeing us. Of course, God's Word says He knows us, but without any real interaction with God we can ignore that fact. Our lack of prayer is a way of "covering our eyes" so He can't see us.

Another reason we often resist a face-to-face encounter with God is that it may point to our need for greater submission in certain areas. Our carnal nature (our natural, earthly desires) will automatically fight against this. It has been in control for a long time and has no intention of giving up without a struggle. And so we find excuses to resist any real intimacy with our heavenly Father.

Only more contact, more communication, and more knowledge of God will break down these barriers to intimacy that reside within the heart of every person. There is a longing for a closer relationship that tugs at us all from time to time, making us pray those prayers of love and dedication to our Father. Yet most of us do not expend a great deal of time and energy in fervent pursuit of God. After we ask Jesus into our lives, we often settle into our own version of Christianity, and, like the children of Israel, content ourselves with knowing God on our terms, in our time, and according to our desires.

But that isn't enough for God. Whether you have a great desire or an apathetic one, God desires for you to know Him with intensity fierce in its pursuit and voluminous in its capacity. God loves you. He has redeemed you at great cost to Himself simply because He wants a relationship with you.

And since God knows nothing will bring us the joy He personally can, He will use the circumstances of our lives to draw us closer to Him. Then as we tentatively begin to experience God when we cry out to Him for help, our hearts will begin to be caught by Him.

Learning to Pray

A consistent prayer relationship brings the knowledge we have of God into experience in our lives so that we not only know about God, we know Him; we don't just know about His great love for us, but we experience it personally. When this happens, God is no longer a distant deity but rather a personal friend, and we begin to experience all the freedom and joy that knowing God and being known by Him was meant to bring.

Although we do desire a better prayer life at times, we've probably tried and failed repeatedly to be more consistent. Problems drive us to God, but usually, when the need is gone, so is the motivation to pray. We soon fall back into the same pattern as before. It seems to be a universal trait that we don't seek God with as much fervency and desire when things are going well.

It may only be when the desire to pray and the desire for a closer relationship with God becomes strong enough to force us to despair of ever getting any better at it that we will be ready to learn how to pray.

> Call to me and I will answer you and tell you great and unsearchable things you do not know.
> —Jeremiah 33:3

Reflect

Have you been "covering your eyes" to hide from God?

Has fear of *being known* kept you from pursuing a more intimate relationship with Jesus?

God's desire for intimacy with you has its roots in His unconditional love for you. Some of us, because of past failings or difficult relationships, have trouble accepting God's love. We "hide our eyes" because of insecurity and fear of rejection.

Spend some time today asking God to show you if you hide from Him. Realize that because of Christ's work on the cross, nothing has to stay the same. Whatever kept you from pursuing a close relationship with God in the past no longer has to be a hindrance as you learn to receive the help of the Holy Spirit in this area of your life.

Study

How does Hagar describe God in Genesis 16:13?

_____

_____

In Jeremiah 23:23-24, what does God say about people hiding from Him?

_____

_____

Fear of being known is not the only reason for keeping God at a distance. Are there areas of your life you want to keep off limits to God?

Think about this question honestly. Write down whatever areas come to mind.

_____

_____

_____

Prayer of Response

Spend a few minutes talking to God right now about how you feel about being known by Him.

Verbalize your feelings out loud, realizing He is with you and He is listening.

Ask the Lord to show you and help you dismantle any "off limits" areas of your life. Start with the prayer below, but then use your own words to tell God that you want your prayer life to be different.

Dear Father God,

I have been guilty of hiding from You by not coming to You in prayer. Forgive me for my fear, my reluctance to know and be known by You. Help me to be different. Fill my heart with Your Spirit and enable me to pray....

Receiving God's Love

Look up and underline in your Bible each of the following verses. Personalize each one by writing your name or the word "me" above the words "world," "we," and "us" or after the word "you."

John 3:16   Romans 5:8
I John 3:1   Jeremiah 31:3

Each day this week, use one of these scriptures at the end of your time of prayer. Tell God you love Him and read one of the scriptures out loud, using your own name or a personal pronoun.

Wait quietly in His presence after you read the verse. Consciously choose to receive God's love. Don't worry about whether or not you feel loved. You are choosing to believe the Word of God about His love for you.

Discussion

Share any problems you may have had with receiving God's love.

CHAPTER 4

A New Control

After living in apartments and smaller homes we were able to purchase a larger house, and one of the items that came with it was a new garage door opener. I had never had one and quickly learned to appreciate the extra steps it saved me. However, the little control I kept in my car didn't really work as well as I would have liked. It seemed to have a mind of its own and would open the door only after I had pushed, turned, shaken, and mauled it for an indeterminate length of time.

Whenever I drove up our driveway or out of the garage, I would stop, pick up the control, aim it at the garage door, and press the button, hoping it would work on the first try. It rarely did. I would press it again and again, holding it this way and that, trying every angle. Then all of a sudden, the door would open (or close), and I was left wondering what I had done that made it work this time.

I would, from time to time, think I had found just the right way to hold it or just the right way to push the button for it to work consistently—only to have that "way" fail after working for me for a week or so.

Then there were the days it never did work—when I had to get out of the car and climb the fence to get into the garage or, when I was leaving, walk back into the garage, use the wall control by the door into the house, and then run as fast as I could to get out before the garage door came down on top of me. I can't count the times I slipped going under it at the last minute and sprawled onto the ground.

Often, if the kids were in the car when I couldn't get it to work, one of them would take the control and press on it. Sometimes it would be passed all around the car until "presto," all of a sudden, it worked! Then whoever had the control would smugly say, "See, you just have to press the button on the right side (or the left, or in the middle)" or "You just have to hold it this way (or that way)." We all had our pet theories of what made the control work.

What really amazes me is how patiently I put up with all this. I just got used to having a faulty garage door opener. I knew I couldn't count on it to work all the time, but I had never known anything better, so I really didn't give it much thought. It worked enough of the time that I knew it was better than not having a garage door opener at all.

Whenever Chuck drove the car, however, he would get totally upset about it. This didn't happen very often because we usually rode in his car when all of us were together, so he seldom had to use it. My little control frustrated him completely. "This is ridiculous! How can you stand this? This doesn't work right at all!"

I would usually end up defending it. After all, it was all I had, and it usually worked…eventually.

That was the problem. It worked just enough to keep me from doing anything about it. Just about the time I was totally frustrated, it would work well again for a while. I continued to put up with it, even on those days it didn't function, because I knew it would eventually work again.

After about two years of this, Chuck's car was being serviced, so we all piled into mine to go somewhere. "Zap," the garage door shut with just one touch of the control. However, when we came home and pulled into the driveway, Chuck reached for the control, pressed the button, and…nothing happened. Big surprise. He pressed it a few more times until I said, "Here, give it to me."

I proceeded to hold it in all sorts of positions, aiming and pushing the button. It still didn't work. Matt reached up from the backseat to take it. He twisted and shook it, but after a few tries, he handed it back.

Chuck grabbed it and tried again, getting more and more frustrated, muttering and shaking the control more and more violently. Finally, he got out of the car, threw the control on the ground, and stomped on it. He then picked up all the pieces, calmly walked over to the garbage can, and threw them in.

A New Control

He came back to the car, sent Matt to open the garage door, and said, "I'll buy you a new one today."

Do you know that there are actually garage door controls that work all the time, every time you use them? Amazing! I had appreciated mine even though it worked only sporadically. I might have lived with that garage door control indefinitely.

How often our prayer life is just like that little control. It works enough to make us appreciate its value, but a lot of the time it just frustrates us.

As Christians, we've learned that one fundamental of the Christian faith is prayer. Intellectually, we know prayer is the answer to our needs; it is the answer to our problems, and it is necessary if we are to live a victorious Christian life.

We know prayer is the "control" that opens the way to many things, but our personal "control" just doesn't seem to work very well. Other people tell us, "This is the way to pray," or, "The key is to_____," but we aren't sure why God seems to answer this prayer and not that one. We wish we could be more consistent and have a prayer life like other people we know, but we just seem to continue, year after year, in the same pattern. We hope for the best and often wonder,

"Will it work this time?"
"Will God answer my prayer?"
"Do I have enough faith to receive an answer?"
"Will I finally become more disciplined in prayer?"

We need someone like Chuck to come along, take our prayer life, and smash it to the ground. We need something or someone to make us realize how pathetic our faulty prayer life really is and, at the same time, hold out the promise of a new control that really works—one that is consistent, rooted in faith, and will open the door into God's presence every time!

I don't know what it will take for you to finally despair of your personal prayer life enough to throw it on the ground. But part of the "smashing" process is coming to realize our own part in the problem, our willingness to put up with the prayer life we've had all along. When we become honest about this and our heart becomes caught in the desire for a real prayer relationship, God has a "new control" for us.

Our part is to admit we are unable in ourselves to be disciplined enough to carry out an effective prayer life day after day. If we're honest, we have to admit that every day (unless there is a pressing need) there is a reluctance, a dread, a putting off, when it comes to spending time in prayer. It may be just a small holding back; it may be a feeling of lethargy. It may be wanting to pray, but "later," or it may be a strong wish not to bother with it at all.

Even those who have become disciplined in praying daily may still be giving God only their "duty" prayers; enough to fulfill some sort of personal requirement, but without any motivation to come any closer. If they are honest with themselves, there still may be a reluctance to spend any time or energy pursuing a real encounter with God.

We can become pretty adept at covering up this reluctance with all sorts of excuses. Usually it is something we can justify pretty easily: busyness. We tell ourselves we really don't have the time to come into God's presence. We would love to, *but...*

This reluctance is part of our carnal nature, which is still fighting for its right to be the dominant force in our life. A consistent prayer life and a more intimate relationship with God are real threats to its power. The only way we can deal effectively with the reluctance our carnality generates is to acknowledge it. To realize that until we die, our carnal nature will resist in some measure coming into submission to the Spirit of God within us.

Recognizing this reluctance and repenting of it is another step in learning to pray.

> You will seek me and find me when you seek me with all your heart.
> —Jeremiah 29:13

Reflect

If you despair of ever having a consistent, meaningful prayer life, but your desire is to walk with God and know Him, you are in the perfect position to receive His help and strength.

A New Control

Write down how much time you spend in prayer now.

How do you feel about prayer? Do you ever question its value?

Have you been frustrated at your lack of consistency?

Examine where you are in your willingness to spend time in prayer, or to come to God wholeheartedly and honestly.

Study

According to Psalm 65:4, where does the desire to pray come from?

_____

What does God promise to do in Isaiah 41:10?

_____

What is the common assurance of the following verses?

    Isaiah 40:29

    2 Corinthians 12:9

    Psalm 138:3

_____

Look up:

    1 Thessalonians 5:23-24

    James 1:17

    Jude 24

Who is responsible for the good we are called to do?_____

According to 1 Corinthians 15:10, how was Paul able to labor so abundantly?

_____

Learning to Pray

In Philippians 2:12-13, how are we to work out our own salvation?

_____

The fear and trembling come when we become aware of our inadequacy. What are we promised in verse 13?

_____

Receiving God's Help

Read Isaiah 41:8-20 several times. Underline the portions that promise help and any others that speak to you personally.

Write your name after some of the "you" words. (Example: "You are my servant. I have chosen you, [Deborah]..." verse 9.)

In the space below, or in your prayer diary, write out a prayer asking God for help. Begin by writing down a confession of your personal problems with prayer. Acknowledge the sin in your life that has kept you from having a vibrant, consistent, intimate prayer life, then write out your request for help.

_____

_____

_____

_____

Prayer of Response

This would be a good time to memorize and add to your life the Jesus Prayer:

> "Lord Jesus Christ, Son of God, have mercy on me, a sinner."

A New Control

This prayer phrase, from the second century desert fathers, has been used by countless spiritual pilgrims throughout the centuries as a way to cry out for help during the day and as a way to begin formal prayer times. Each element is important. With this prayer, we proclaim the deity of Jesus, and by calling upon Him, we acknowledge Him as the way to the Father. Also, it is an elemental cry for help and an acknowledgment of our sin nature which constantly needs forgiveness, mercy, and help.

Discussion

Share any problems or frustration you have had with prayer.

What do you think of the Jesus Prayer? Was it helpful to you?

> *The best prayer in the world is only two words, "Help me," when it comes from the heart.*
> —Thomas Keating

CHAPTER 5

Help

When my daughter was in junior high, she brought a friend named Natalie home several times for slumber parties and other get-togethers. Because Natalie was quiet and shy, with an eagerness to please and a sweet, compassionate temperament, she stood out from the rest of the rowdy, gossipy, fun-loving seventh and eighth graders who were usually around.

When I asked about her, my kids quickly began to tell me her story. "Wow, Mom, she rides the commuter train from Oakland every day and then she has to walk all the way to the school from the station!" Jula and Matt thought walking to the corner store was an ordeal, so Natalie's walk from her home to the station, her 30-minute ride to our town, the 2-mile walk to school, and then the same trip in reverse seemed pretty awesome to them.

"And," my son continued, "she brings her younger brother three days a week to preschool, and she has to carry him most of the way back and forth."

I talked to the teacher later and found out that both of Natalie's parents worked full-time, and she had two brothers under five, so quite a bit was required of her. Although they didn't live in a bad section of the city, her parents still didn't want Natalie attending school there. Many of her afterschool hours were spent babysitting, and when one of her little brothers started preschool she was also in charge of getting him there and back.

My daughter complained at times when Natalie couldn't come over to spend the night or when she couldn't participate in various activities. She felt Natalie's parents were mean. I would try to remind her that even though Natalie had more responsibility than most kids, her parents did love her and were doing what they felt was best. Everyone tried to include Natalie as much as possible, and she was so appreciative when she could be in on the fun.

As the end of the school year drew closer, everyone began to look forward to the last week of school and their annual day at an amusement park similar to Six Flags. It was always a special day for everyone. Students, teachers, and chaperoning parents traveled together in two big buses, singing songs and laughing and talking about what they would do. At the park they rode the rides (the Tidal Wave, the Grizzly, the Big Dipper, and the "Edge"), screaming in fear and teasing the ones who were chicken! Everyone watched the magic shows and the musical revues, ate hot dogs and popcorn and cotton candy, and tried to do as much as possible in one day.

Then they all piled into the buses, a little sick from the rides and exhausted from the walking, but still excited over the fun. On the ride home everyone talked at once, trying to tell what they had done and reliving the best moments: "Did you see...?" "I nearly died when..."

It was always a fun day and everyone wanted to go. All the students worked hard to raise money to pay for the buses and tickets with bake sales, carnivals, and various fundraisers. Excitement over the trip mounted as it drew closer, and when the big day arrived my kids were ready for it! "The buses will leave at 8:00 sharp, Mom, and we're supposed to be there early!"

They scurried around trying to get ready in spite of my interruptions: "You've got to eat breakfast." "Don't forget your lunch money." "Did you get your jacket?" Still, we arrived in plenty of time. The kids hurried to get a good seat on the bus, waving excitedly from the window. Soon the buses were pulling away from the parking lot.

But there was one student missing...Natalie. The principal had waited as long as possible, but she'd finally had to tell the bus drivers to go ahead. Only a few minutes later Natalie ran into the driveway, looked around at the empty schoolyard, and burst into tears. She went into the office, sobbing as if her heart would break, trying to explain to the school secretary that her train had been late.

The secretary listened while Natalie described her wait at the station, watching the minutes tick by as she slowly realized that she would be late. Fighting the tears, Natalie just kept hoping, and when the train

Help

finally arrived and she started on her way, she kept looking at her watch and wishing the train would go faster.

After she arrived at the station, she got off the train and began to run. As fast as she could, she ran the mile and a half to the school, but when she turned the corner into the yard she saw the buses were gone and...Her voice trailed off as she stood there crying.

The secretary walked around her desk and put her arms around Natalie, comforting her as best as she could and thinking, *How unfair. Of all the kids, she deserved to enjoy this day.*

The secretary's husband, Jim, a highway patrol officer, happened to walk into the office at that moment and immediately wanted to know what was wrong. As his wife related the story, he looked at the distraught girl, and before the story was finished he grabbed her arm and said, "Come on."

He hurried Natalie out to his patrol car, told her to put on her seat belt, and took off. Radioing ahead to fellow officers, he described the buses and told the officers what highway they were on and the direction they were traveling. About ten minutes later, a highway patrolman pulled over two big yellow buses and asked the principal to step out.

"What's the matter? What's happened?" she asked, bewildered and a little frightened.

"I don't know, ma'am. I was just told to hold the bus."

A few minutes later Jim came roaring up in his patrol car, sliding to a stop in the gravel behind the other officer's car. When Natalie stepped out and ran toward the bus, the principal realized what had happened and started laughing. The kids all began to cheer and, grinning from ear to ear, Natalie turned to wave goodbye to her rescuer before hurrying up the steps into the bus to join her friends.

How many times have you wished for someone to rescue you when you've tried your best but still seemed to miss out? Sometimes it's like that in our Christian walk. Over and over, our own carnality slows us down. We despair of ever getting better. We feel it is hopeless. We don't seem to have any control over our own lives. In the area of prayer, there seems to be no way to be consistent. We try and try, only to fail. And even those who doggedly keep a disciplined prayer time going may still wonder if it's doing any good.

Learning to Pray

We simply fail to understand that there is someone to help us, just like the highway patrol officer helped Natalie. The Holy Spirit of God is waiting to help you and I come into the presence of God. He knows exactly what is needed in each of our lives and exactly how to get us there.

God wants you to pray. It is the fervent desire of His heart. And God knows how to help you to pray, no matter how undisciplined, lazy, inconsistent, discouraged, or unbelieving you may be. Even a little step on your part will open the floodgates of God's divine enablement to you.

Once we have admitted our own part in the problem, and perhaps begun to despair of getting better, we are ready to receive the help of our own "highway patrol officer" who is waiting to get us to the place we so desire to be.

In my little analogy, the highway patrolman is an excellent picture of the Holy Spirit, given to help usher us into the presence of God. But in truth He is with us already. Our problem is we have not yet learned to use the help God has provided. So we struggle along on our own, never fully realizing that God intends for prayer to be something different altogether than what we perhaps have thought, and that He has provided for us a constant helper to bring us into His presence and to teach us how to pray:

> But the Counselor, the Holy Spirit, whom the Father will send in my name, will teach you all things and will remind you of everything I have said to you.
>
> —John 14:26

We need to remember that the grace by which we were saved is the same grace in which we will continue to walk throughout our Christian life:

> Are you so foolish? After beginning with the Spirit, are you now trying to attain your goal by human effort?
>
> —Galatians 3:3

Help

> So then, just as you received Christ Jesus as Lord, continue to live in him.
>
> —Colossians 2:6

The Christian life is an extension of what happened at salvation. God extended grace to you through Jesus. He reached out and offered eternal life, forgiveness of sins, and a relationship with Him.

You needed only to say yes, to reach out and receive what God offered. You didn't need anything else. You didn't need brains, a strong will, talent, or self-discipline. You needed only to accept God's gift.

Every part of our Christian life, from salvation to eternity in heaven, is simply a matter of receiving what God has provided each new step of the way, whether it is help in overcoming sin, receiving principles and truth from God's Word, or establishing a prayer life. It is a continual receiving of God's grace and His divine enablement:

> His divine power has given us everything we need for life and godliness.
>
> —2 Peter 1:3

It is obvious that we do have to physically carry out the responsibilities of a Christian and do the things God asks of us if we are to have a meaningful relationship with Him. In the matter of prayer, this means I will have to make time to pray and then do it! And you might say, "Yes, and that is the hard part!" We don't feel capable of carrying this out day after day.

The key is recognizing we are not capable and asking for help. The Holy Spirit is God's help given to us. Our part is to give Him control of our lives.

"Okay," you may say. "But what do I do?'

We have to start with the basics, admitting we need God's help to pray as we should, and then asking for that help every day. We do it simply by saying:

> "Draw me to You, Father."
> "Help me to pray today, God."
> "Teach me to pray."

These simple phrases are really a form of the first line in the Lord's Prayer. "Thy kingdom come, Thy will be done." We are asking for God's will to be done in us.

When I utter the words, "Lord, help me with this," I am admitting I can't do it on my own. I am giving over my will to the Spirit of God who resides in me. That frees Him to change my heart-attitude, so that I want to do the thing I was dreading.

When I was first trying to develop a disciplined prayer life, I tried and failed repeatedly to be consistent. One day I'd be emotionally charged and ready to pray, but three days later I would be saying things such as:

"I got to bed late so I can't get up early."
"It's too late now; I don't have time."
"I've got too much to do."

I found that after a few days of excuses, I would begin to ignore thoughts about prayer. That was when I decided to pray about praying. Seems strange, doesn't it? But I had to admit I was helpless to help myself. I had recently learned the truth of Romans 6 with regard to overcoming sin (how when I died with Christ my sinful nature died, too, and how I needed to realize that Christ in me is stronger than my propensity to sin). That understanding made me certain that God could accomplish this too.

However, when I began to "pray about praying," God didn't pick me up out of bed in the mornings and throw me on the floor, saying, "Now get started!" No, as I began to say to God in just a sentence or so, "Lord, I need to pray today and I don't want to; please give me the strength to do it anyway," the desire to pray would become stronger than the desire not to pray.

I would usually pray that little sentence prayer as soon as I got up. Then I would go ahead and start my day. While I was fixing lunches and getting the day started for everyone else, I would perhaps pray it again.

Coming to God regularly in prayer became easier and easier as time went on. But if I missed praying for a while because of sickness or

Help

vacations, it was hard to start again. Then I would pray like I had in the beginning. Just a sentence or two—but that was all that was necessary. My cry for help opened the door to the Spirit of God within me to help me to do the thing that was vital to my Christian life.

Recently, I read an article about a young man who was struggling with alcoholism. In relating his story, he told about a day he was alone in his house:

> I was really fighting a drink and about ready to give in when I fell to my knees, something I hadn't done since I was a kid. "God," I prayed aloud, "give me strength, give me faith. Show me that You'll see me through this." Suddenly I didn't really want that drink. I didn't know what I wanted. I didn't even know for sure if I believed God was there or if He heard me—but I didn't drink that day.

We've heard these kinds of testimonies many times, but how often we fail to grasp that the same power available to help people who cry out in need for deliverance from drugs, alcohol, and sin is also available daily to help us pray!

When we're ready to be helped with prayer, God is waiting to help us. Like the highway patrol officer who helped Natalie get to her destination, God has already provided all we need through the Holy Spirit, who was given to help us to pray.

Day after day, as we whisper the words, "Help me to pray," God begins to call our hearts to Him. Then He enables us, through the Spirit of God within us, to take dominion over the flesh until our relationship with Him is developed enough for our prayer life to be a pleasure to be enjoyed, rather than a matter for vacillation, guilt, or dutiful drudgery.

> For the grace of God that brings salvation has appeared to all men. It teaches us to say "No" to ungodliness and worldly passions, and to live *self-controlled*, upright and godly lives in this present age.
> —Titus 2:11-12, emphasis added

> For God did not give us a spirit of timidity, but a spirit of power, of love, and of *self-discipline*.
> —2 Timothy 1:7, emphasis added

Learning to Pray

Asking for God's help is the key that brings the divine enablement we need. There are exciting, rewarding, and intimate times of fellowship with God ahead for each of us as He opens Himself to us in relationship and we open ourselves to Him. Our intimacy with God will deepen as we begin to seek God for His help in our prayer life, as we learn to cry out, "Help me, Father, to pray."

> How gracious he will be when you cry for help! As soon as he hears, he will answer you.
> —Isaiah 30:19

Reflect

> *Matthew 11:28 says "Come to me." His word come means "to act." Yet the last thing we want to do is come. But everyone who does come knows that, at that very moment, the supernatural power of the life of God invades him. The dominating power of the world, the flesh, the devil is now paralyzed; not by your act, but because your act has joined you to God and tapped you in to His redemptive power."*
> —Oswald Chambers (My Utmost for His Highest)

Do you have a problem with self-discipline, especially in the area of the Christian disciplines of prayer, Bible reading, etc?

Are you struggling right now to overcome habitual sin or self-destructive habits or lifestyles?

Has life as a Christian just seemed too hard?

Whatever sin, habit, or problem you may be struggling with, whether it relates to your sin nature, your lack of will power or lack of self discipline—*Jesus in you is more powerful than whatever you are struggling against.*

Help

Our Lord's Cross is the gateway into His life. His resurrection means that He has the power to convey His life to me. When I was born again, I received the very life of the risen Lord from Jesus Himself.
—Oswald Chambers

Study

What does each of the following verses promise?

Philippians 1:6 _____

1 Corinthians 1:4-9 _____

2 Corinthians 9:8 _____

These promises are based on the work of Jesus Christ: His incarnation, His death, and His resurrection. I am praying that as you read and meditate on the following scriptures, you will understand as you never have before what Christ's death and resurrection means to you personally.

Read 1 Peter 2:24 and write it out:

_____

_____

Read Romans 6:1-11. In your own words, what does this mean to you?

_____

_____

Jesus' death and resurrection and the difference it makes in our lives is fact. However, we must believe it in order to walk in victory over the sin nature. When we realize and count on (reckon, consider) the fact that Jesus in us is greater than our carnal nature, we will be free from our struggles to live a Christian life on our own. Then we can rest in Christ's ability to accomplish in us those things that will please Him.

Learning to Pray

It doesn't matter how weak or vacillating you think you are because *God is in you!*

What assurance are we given in John 14:23?

_____

_____

Receiving God's Help

Read Psalm 138:8. What does it promise?

_____

_____

God will not *make* you do anything, but He will *enable* you to do all that is required to live a life of peace, joy, and obedience to His plans and purposes for you. He will help you to pray.

Pick one of the scripture promises from this lesson or the last and memorize it.

Prayer of Response

Dear Jesus,

Thank You again for dying for me on the cross. I realize that my sin nature—including my inconsistent, apathetic, and faithless response to Your call to prayer—was with You on that cross. I am no longer controlled by it, but by Your life in me.

Thank You, Jesus, for Your faithfulness to *complete* Your work in me.

Amen.

Help

Discussion

Discuss Romans 6:1-14 and whether or not you were helped by it.

Share which scripture you chose to memorize and why.

Be prepared to quote your scripture.

Prayer and helplessness are inseparable. Only he who is helpless can truly pray. Your helplessness is your best prayer. It calls from your heart to the heart of God with greater effect than all your uttered pleas.
—Ole Hallesby (Prayer)

CHAPTER 6

Getting Started

The day I made Jula cry in my attempt to motivate her to practice the piano, I realized I would have to do more than just set a new piece of music in front of her and bribe her to master it. So the next day I sat with her at the piano and began to break the song down into easier sections. I showed her just the right hand of the first page and had her practice that. In a few days we added the left hand. Then we moved on to the second page. Soon she had gone far enough to realize she could learn it. It wasn't an impossible task anymore; it was something within her reach.

Even after seeing how much God desires fellowship with us and the help He has provided through His Spirit, daily prayer may still seem overwhelming. Before we look at prayer in much more detail, it might be helpful to outline some simple, practical steps on how to get started.

1. *Ask God to give you the desire to develop a closer relationship with Him.* This includes a desire to read and study God's Word and a desire to spend time in prayer. Even if you are already disciplined about praying, you should still be asking for God to draw you closer.
2. *Ask God to help you begin to set aside time.* Some days you will have more time than others. The amount of time each day is not the key. The important thing is that you reserve time for God, just for Him, out of your life.

    Don't try to begin with an hour. Start with 10 to 20 minutes. As you begin to develop your relationship with God, you will want to spend more time with Him. You'll have more to talk about as He becomes your intimate friend.

3. *Start by using the simple ACTS formula.* This formula divides your prayer time into four distinct segments, helping you become familiar with the different facets of prayer even as you are initially learning to pray. ACTS stands for *adoration, confession, thanksgiving, and supplication.*

Adoration
Begin simply by thanking and praising God for who He is. You might want to sing a song or hymn that expresses worship. You could also focus on one attribute of God's character: His mercy, compassion, loving kindness, etc.

Confession
Use this time to confess before God any sins you know you have committed. We will discuss repentance in detail later, but there is always a need for daily examination. When Jesus washed the disciples' feet and Peter said, "No Lord, not my feet," Jesus answered, "Then you can have no part of me."

Peter replied quickly, "Then wash all of me," and Jesus instructed him, "No, you only need your feet washed."

Jesus was referring to the daily dust we pick up as we walk through life: the harsh word spoken in haste, the impatient attitude shown toward the store clerk who was doing his best, the misleading words we used to throw someone off the truth, our self-centered choices.

Sin comes between God and us. It interferes with our communion with Him and is sometimes the reason God does not answer our prayers. We need to routinely ask God to examine our hearts for any sin that might be lurking there. Psalm 66:18 says, "If I regard iniquity in my heart, the Lord will not hear me" (KJV).

Thanksgiving
Use this time to express appreciation to God for the specific things He has done for you. We need to thank Him for His answers to prayer and the help He gives.

Getting Started

Supplication
Now spend some time bringing your requests to God. He knows your heart and is very aware of your needs and desires, but you need to come and ask. God can do nothing but in response to prayer. Begin right away to bring other people's needs to God, as well as your own.

This is a simple, effective way to get started, but I hope you won't become tied to it. It's only a help, not the eleventh commandment!

The Holy Spirit within us will help us. As we ask for help in getting started, He begins to draw us to pray. He will also begin to show us daily what God's design and purpose is for that day so we can pray in His will. Here are some additional thoughts on quiet times with God.

Spend time reading the Bible. Ask the Lord to direct you in choosing where to read. Many people like to read a psalm or a chapter in Proverbs while they read through the other books in the Old and New Testaments.

Pray out loud. It helps you formulate your thoughts and also keeps your mind from wandering. Learn to spend time talking to God about your day, what's bothering you, what makes you happy, and anything else you want to share. Remember, God wants to establish a relationship with you and is interested in your life.

Consider starting a prayer diary. Use it to write letters to God, to keep lists of requests and answers, to record truths you have recently learned, or things you feel God is saying to you. Let it reflect your innermost thoughts. Sometimes it is easier to write things down than to say them. A prayer diary will help keep you disciplined because it is a record of your devotional life.

Change your prayer location from time to time. Go outside in the spring. Sit by the fireplace when it's cold. Have coffee at the kitchen table. I love the sunshine, so I tend to follow it during the year as it moves to shine through different windows.

On the days you really can't get away for a few minutes of quiet time, it is important to verbally give yourself and your day to God.

"Father, I give myself to You today. Guide my footsteps and help me to walk in Your will."

Develop the habit of praising God all during the day. Just a phrase or two of worship, a whispered prayer for help at times of need, thanksgiving for the good things that happen, and praise in spite of the bad will bring pleasure to God and also help you tremendously.

Christian books are a great resource! If you have time, read one along with the Bible during your quiet time. But books should never replace the Word. And don't fall into the trap of using Christian TV as a substitute for a personal prayer time. It isn't the same at all!

Music (perhaps some praise and worship cds) can be extremely beneficial in helping you to focus more completely on God. Use it to help you in your time of worship as you are beginning to pray.

Developing a close relationship with God is a *great adventure*. No matter how often you may fail to keep up with your personal time of devotion, try again. It does start out as a discipline, but God will help you. A willing heart is the key.

> My heart has heard you say, "Come and talk with me, O my people."
> And my heart responds, "Lord, I am coming."
> —Psalm 27:8 TLB

Reflect

> *The truth is, we only learn to pray all the time everywhere after we have resolutely set about praying some of the time somewhere.*
> —John Dalrymple (Simple Prayer)

Whatever type of prayer life you are hanging onto right now, please be willing to grow and change. Ask God to give you a desire for growth in the area of prayer.

Some of you reading this book may have developed a habit of praying on the go. You may actually get a lot of praying done this way and I am not trying to discourage the continuation of that; however, the above quote is true for you, too. There is resident in that kind of prayer life a subtle, yet real, attempt to keep God at a distance we are comfortable with. Prayer needs to become much more than what it perhaps has been for each of us; we need to begin to walk in the fullness of an intimate, life-sharing relationship with God that will only be forged through daily appointments with Him and time set aside for Him. If this is the only kind of praying you do, please make a commitment to begin setting aside time for focused prayer.

Practical Steps

Decide when (what time of day) you can be most consistent. For most people, it will be first thing in the morning. That means getting up earlier. This is where your desire for intimacy and fellowship with God meets with reality. Hopefully, you have begun to recognize and deal with your own unwillingness, laziness, or lack of desire by admitting to it and asking for help.

You need to examine your life and schedule ruthlessly. What do you do instead of going to bed early enough to be able to get up for a prayer time? Do you spend a lot of time on the phone? Do you watch TV or read late at night? God understands our need for rest and recreation, but learn to put Him first. I promise that as you do, He will provide rest for you.

You may want to ask God to help you decide on a time if you have small children or an irregular schedule. When my children were small, I couldn't always count on the time they would get up, so I scheduled my quiet time during their naps.

(You may also want to give yourself permission to make Saturday or Sunday your Sabbath from the discipline of a quiet time if your family schedule makes it hard to accommodate it. However, make God a part of your life in a different way on that day, perhaps by having a prayer time with your children around the breakfast table.)

Write down the time of day you have chosen:_____

Try to find someone who will encourage you in your new commitment to prayer, and ask if they will keep you accountable for the next few months.

Study

What promise does Philippians 2:13 have for you today?_____

_____

Circle the word "works." The Greek word is *energeo*. It means energizes or empowers.

Look up 2 Timothy 1:7 in your Bible.

If your Bible uses the term "sound mind," write "self-discipline" next to it. The Greek word *sophronismos* is more accurately translated self-control or self-discipline.

Receiving God's Help

Write your name over the word "us" in the above scripture and spend some time thinking about what that means to you.

In 2 Peter 1:3-4, write your name above the word "us" and meditate on that scripture. (Meditation means to contemplate or reflect. Let every facet of its meaning penetrate your heart)

Ask God to make each of the above scriptures real to you, and to give you faith to receive from Him the sufficiency and self discipline you need.

Prayer of Response

Dear Father,

I ask for help. Jesus, You are greater than my inconsistency and I receive Your work in my life. Holy Spirit, I ask You to draw me each day to pray, and I ask You to empower me each day with Your spirit of self-discipline.

Amen.

My Prayer for You

Dear Father God,

At this moment of commitment, I pray for the one reading this book. I have experienced the up-and-down path to a regular committed prayer time and I have received Your enabling dear Holy Spirit. Now I ask You to impart it to _____.

See their desire. Fill them, draw them, enable them, and keep them steadfast on the path to intimate relationship with You and a consistent prayer life.

Jesus, our Savior, Redeemer, Helper, and Friend, You are with them at this moment and You are praying for them. Give them that awareness as You do Your work in them.

In Your name, Jesus.

Amen.

Discussion

Share honestly about some of your struggles with disciplined prayer, both now and in the past.

Relate some of your own prayer techniques, habits, or discoveries. Share anything that helped you learn to be consistent.

Tell your group about whatever commitment you made to prayer. Make yourself accountable to one another for a few months. At the beginning of each week of study, share how you are doing and pray for one another.

LEARNING FROM GOD

Take my yoke upon you and learn from me.
—Matthew 11:29

CHAPTER 7

Face to Face with God

David and Goliath. Who hasn't heard the story? A small shepherd boy standing against a giant with a slingshot and a handful of rocks.... it's a classic tale of good versus evil, of courage in the face of overwhelming odds, of youthful enthusiasm and dreams, and of the power of faith in God.

When the story is told, the speaker usually goes into great detail describing the events leading up to this incident, David's stature in relationship to the giant, his past exploits, his brothers' derogatory comments, and the boasting of Goliath. The speaker may then talk about David's faith in God or Saul's attempt to help David by giving him his armor, and the story usually ends with the victory over Goliath. But that isn't really the end.

The Bible goes on to give a sort of postscript or epilogue. It says, "David took the Philistine's head and brought it to Jerusalem, *and he put the Philistine's weapons in his own tent*" (1 Samuel 17:54, emphasis added).

David kept Goliath's armor. The sermons we hear on David and Goliath don't usually mention it, but the armor was David's trophy, gained through an incredible experience, and he wanted to keep it. He wanted something tangible to look at and remember the supernatural victory God had given him.

I wonder if David somehow knew, when he decided to save the weapons, how important the armor might become in the future.

David soon became a part of Saul's court. He received a commission into Saul's army, and everything the king gave him to do, he accomplished successfully. He married Saul's daughter, and Saul's son, Jonathan, became his closest friend. During these heady and wonderful times, David may have forgotten about the armor. He was experiencing success; he didn't need to dwell on past victories.

However, David's military exploits gradually brought an end to his favored status. Saul grew jealous and fearful of David's popularity. He began to look for ways to get rid of him, and his attempts finally forced David into exile.

The day David fled from Saul's presence he had to leave so quickly that he didn't have time to even grab a weapon. However, when he stopped to rest at the temple at Nob, he asked the priest there for a sword or spear. The priest said to him, "We don't have any weapons here. Well, wait a minute. There is one. We have Goliath's sword, wrapped in an ephod. You could have that."

Can you imagine David's delight—his old trophy, back in his hands again, at a time when he needed armor and at a time when he desperately needed to remember God's faithfulness to him.

The next ten years of David's life were filled with hardships and troubles. Constantly on the move, his life continually threatened, separated from his wife and closest friend, David's successful life had abruptly changed into one of desperation and adversity.

And yet, when events pushed him toward despair—when he wondered if God was really on his side or he became so discouraged he could hardly keep going—David could walk into his tent and there would be Goliath's sword. In looking at this physical representation of God's favor and blessing, I'm sure he could remember the feelings of apprehension mingled with belief before meeting Goliath in battle, yet the presence of the sword was proof that God had not failed him.

That armor resting in the corner of his tent—the sword, ready to be used if needed—would remind him repeatedly that God is faithful to accomplish what He says, that God in us is more powerful than any foe, and that no matter what the circumstances look like, God can be trusted.

Perhaps David showed the sword to the other men around the campfire, retelling the story of that great victory, reliving again the glorious feelings of triumph and joy.

It was an important memory, carrying with it knowledge of God not learned in the reading and memorization of the law. The armor represented a victory, a time when he knew that God's hand was upon him. Just as his experiences with the bear and lion had given him faith to believe God would help him against Goliath, so the sword continued to give him faith in God when circumstances looked bleak.

David knew God's faithfulness and ability to deliver (the sword was a physical representation of it) because he had a history with Him, a history of talking to God and seeing and knowing His involvement in his life.

You and I, just like David, need some armor in our tent. We need experiences with God.

The children of Israel often erected monuments to commemorate events. Jacob set up a pillar when he had a vision of angels. Moses built an altar when the Israelites made a covenant with God.

When the Israelites crossed the Jordan into the Promised Land, God told them to set up an altar of 12 stones to be a memorial forever. God wanted the memory of His participation in their lives to be kept alive!

But what if there are no memories to commemorate? What if we have no history, no memories of past encounters with God, or so few that it is hard for us to say that we really know Him? When our relationship with God is based solely on what we have heard and read about Him, then we have not yet begun to experience Him for ourselves. We don't have any monuments. We don't have any armor.

Knowledge of God through His Word is vital, but eventually that knowledge must be personalized and made an intimate part of our lives so that we don't just know about God, we know *Him*. This history with God, this "knowing" begins in *relational prayer*. As we continue to come to God in prayer, you and I enter into interaction with Him, which leads us into *experiences* of Him that teach us His ways.

Do you see how David received his experience of God? When confronted with a difficulty, he immediately became involved in it with God. Some of us haven't approached God or used our circumstances as an opportunity to involve God in our lives enough to acquire any armor.

We can see from the Psalms that David was a man who knew God in an experiential way. This didn't come about simply by reading the law. David knew God because he spent time with Him and because he had learned to talk to God and know Him.

You and I need more than just "Lord, forgive me for my sins, bless me, and help me" kind of prayers. We need more than a fire-escape kind of relationship with God.

God wants us to know Him in an experiential way. He wants us to have armor for our tents, and this happens as we begin to spend time with Him in relational prayer.

Relational prayer means involving God in every part of our lives. We often begin by involving Him to some degree, but when we don't see an answer to our prayers right away or when God doesn't do things the way we think they should be done, the involvement ends. We assume God isn't interested and we go on, either giving up or pursuing our desires through different means. But relational prayer includes coming to God with our desires and needs in the beginning, and then if our prayer is not answered, coming back again and again. It means coming to God about the matter until we have an answer or until we know what *He* is thinking.

When we have to pray over a matter for any length of time, we are giving God the opportunity to work in our lives, and we are giving ourselves the opportunity to know God, to experience Him.

Watchman Nee calls this experience "dealing with God":

> If anyone wishes to know God he must learn to have transactions with Him. In other words, he needs to *deal with God and to be dealt with by God.* Many Christians carelessly let difficulties or problems pass by without receiving dealings from God. They do not know why He sends them these difficulties. These people may read the Bible daily and seem to possess some knowledge and light, yet they are ignorant of the mind of God. Their knowledge is clearly insufficient. For this cause, beloved, we must deal with God and receive dealings from God; and then shall we truly know Him.

Nee goes on to explain that when we ask for something in prayer and God gives it to us, we have received more than just the thing we asked for; we have received knowledge of God Himself. This comes about as we learn to seek for things from God and then, if we do not receive them, we still continue to ask. Step by step, we can deal with God, coming back again and again until we receive the answer.

The "armor" that we need in our tent is the experience of God that comes from spending time with Him in prayer, confronting Him with our needs and allowing Him to confront us in a one-on-one relationship that grows stronger and more vital each day.

God has more than just answers to give us. He wants to impart spiritual principles to us. He wants to give us understanding, spiritual gifts, and new insight. He wants to focus His cleansing light on us so we can be changed into His image, and He wants to give us intimate knowledge of Himself and His attributes so we will be drawn even closer in our relationship with Him.

Reflect

When we receive an answer to prayer: we have received knowledge of God Himself.
—Watchman Nee (Spiritual Knowledge)

Do you feel you know God well?

Do you want to know Him better...even if it means confrontations, openness, and waiting?

Can you think of desires, needs, or concerns you prayed about for a while, and then stopped because you didn't get an answer or you didn't get the answer you wanted? Did it occur to you to go back to God and talk to Him about it?

What areas of your life have you *not* prayed about?

Study

Read Joshua 4:1-14

What instruction did God give Joshua? (verses 2-3)

Why? (verses 6-7)
_____

What attribute of God was portrayed through this event in Israel's history? (verse 24)_____

According to Judges 2:10, was this memorial (or experience with God) enough for the next generation?_____

What does Psalm 50:15 instruct us to do?
_____

What happens when we do it?
_____

What does Daniel 11:32 (see King James or New American Standard versions, if possible) say about those who know God?
_____

What does Psalm 9:10 say is one benefit of knowing God?_____

How does John 17:3 describe eternal life?_____

Receiving Knowledge of God

Do you have any memories/memorials of God's intervention in your own life?

What quality of God's character has been made known to you because of an experience you went through with God by your side?

> Faithfulness?
> > Grace?
> > > Forgiveness?
> > > > Power?
> > > > > Other?

Assignment

In Chapter 6, the idea of using a prayer diary to help you become more consistent was mentioned. Now we have another reason for its use—as a memorial of God's dealings in your life, and the knowledge of God you gained through those experiences.

If you have not yet done so, I encourage you to get a journal and keep a record of your "dealings" with God. This can be any type of journal, but you may want to get something you can have sections in. That way you can begin to keep track of all the dealings you have with God. You might want to have sections for journaling and writing out prayers, confessions (keep track of the areas God deals with you about that requires repentance and change), intercessory prayer requests and answers, and Scriptures (God's encouragement, guidance, promises, and instructions). If you are like me, however, and aren't very organized, you can just keep it all together.

Prayer of Response

Dear Heavenly Father,

I do want to know You and to experience You in my life. Help me to come and talk to You about *all* my life, to seek You and Your insight, to learn to deal with You, and to open myself up to Your dealings. Forgive me for the many times I have failed to become involved with You during the events of my life. Please help me, Holy Spirit. Be my guide and my help. Thank You for Your loving patience with me.

Amen.

Discussion

Share some "monument" experiences—times you knew God was with you through answered prayer, intervention, divine guidance, etc.

CHAPTER 8

Why We Wait

What about those times when the prayers that we pray so faithfully to God are not answered? We pray, we seek God, and we ask over and over for God to give us our heart's desire, and yet over and over we confront silence.

This kind of struggling in prayer often comes about because of a problem: illness, family situations, career difficulties, or unfulfilled expectations. Whatever the stressful situation may be, it initially brings us to God for help.

Since prayer is God's tool for bringing about a closer relationship, there will be times when He does not grant our requests the moment we utter them. Weeks, months, even years may pass. If we'll continue to come, however, we will discover valuable things about God and about ourselves. Several stories from the Bible relate ways in which this principle works.

Hannah was childless in a time when the lack of children was considered a curse. Her husband loved her dearly, but that was not enough.

As Hannah grew more and more despondent over her inability to bear a child, her husband tried unsuccessfully to cheer her up. "Isn't my love enough?" he would say.

But Hannah wanted a child. She prayed for a child and waited... and prayed and waited. But no answer came.

Finally, in desperation, she went to the temple and wept bitter tears. Then, the Bible says, she made a vow that if God would grant her request and give her a son, she would give him back to God (1 Samuel 1:11).

Hannah's years of crying for a child finally brought her to the point of offering back to God the child she wanted so badly. This would never have happened if Hannah had received an answer to her prayer right away, or if she had refused to keep coming to God.

The child that God gave her was Samuel, the next leader of the Israelite nation. God needed a man to lead Israel to repentance and back to God. He needed a man who would lead the people according to God's direction, and He chose Hannah to accomplish His plan.

God had something in mind when He made Hannah wait for an answer, and God has something in mind when He makes you and I wait. Many times, waiting brings us to the point of surrender. It brings us to a place of teachability or the realization of our need for cleansing. But we reach that point only when we continue in prayer, when we continue to come to God.

Matthew 15:21-28 tells the story of a Canaanite woman who came to Jesus asking for her daughter to be healed. When you read this story, it appears that Jesus didn't want to answer her request and she had to talk Him into it. But it is a good lesson for us in importunity—that is, "dealing with God," coming to Him again and again until we receive an answer. It's also a beautiful example of what we really need being given to us when we keep seeking.

When the Canaanite woman came and asked for healing for her daughter, she was ignored by Jesus (who was also asked by the disciples to send her away). When Jesus finally did answer, He said, "I was sent only to the lost sheep of Israel."

This would be enough rejection for anyone. Most people would have turned away in defeat, but this woman persevered. She tried a new approach. The Scriptures say, "Then she came and knelt before him. 'Lord, help me!' she said."

It was while she was in this position that she really "saw" Jesus. When she came and knelt before Him, she could look into His face, and when she saw Him a connection was made. She was finally able to see her own need, and for the first time she says, "Help me."

This confrontation, this "dealing," brought her into new knowledge of God and of herself.

When Jesus said, "It is not right to take the children's bread and toss it to their dogs," she knew immediately how to answer Him.

"Yes, Lord...but even the dogs eat the crumbs that fall from their masters' table."

Why We Wait

She didn't have this wisdom or this faith in herself. She received it when she came directly to Jesus, when she was in a position to look into His face. It was then that God could deal directly with her, with her need for help. It was at that point that God could reveal His true nature to her, giving her the faith to ask again for the desire of her heart. It was then that she could begin to see what the kingdom of God was really all about so she could participate in a relationship with God.

But often you and I do not want the confrontation. We do not want to wait, and we do not want to keep asking. Yet that is the only way to know God. Prayer is dealing with God. It is coming to Him until we know Him, until we know His voice, and until we become willing to be changed so the relationship can grow. God often delays His answers to our prayers until we are finally desperate enough to throw ourselves at His feet and look into His face.

You may have heard the phrase that God withholds answers from us until we learn to look at His face instead of His hand. That is exactly it. In dealing with God we become willing to come to Him face-to-face, and as we do, He becomes more important to us than the thing for which we are asking. When this happens our response to Him will begin in just a small way to mirror His love, His desire, and His fervor for us.

We "see through a glass darkly," and yet even in our earthly form God wants us to know much more about Him than we do now. He wants us to comprehend much more of His ability to take care of us and His willingness to do so. He wants us to come more and more into the fullness of His love, knowing that as we do, our lives will never be the same. He wants us to gradually learn to be caught up in Him; our life revolving around Him, centered in Him, and fulfilled by Him.

In almost every letter that Paul writes to the churches, he prays for their ability to know God. The most eloquent of these prayers is in Ephesians 3:16-19:

> I pray that out of his glorious riches he may strengthen you with power through his Spirit in your inner being, so that Christ may dwell in your hearts through faith. And I pray that you, being rooted and established in love, may have power, together with all the saints, to grasp how wide and long and high and deep is the love of Christ,

and to know this love that surpasses knowledge—that you may be filled to the measure of all the fullness of God.

Paul understood the need for knowledge of God. He knew that it would make a difference in our lives, giving us the opportunity to experience the intimacy with God that is the very purpose for our existence.

You and I will never come to know God in the way that Paul prays for in Ephesians until we are ready to come to Him in a literal, physical way; until we are ready to deal with Him in a give-and-take relationship; and until we are ready to involve Him in every part of our existence, making possible His participation in our lives.

Different Answers

They're almost unbelievable—
    some prayer answers
You sent so fast
    they took my breath away
And made me laugh.
I thank You.

I thank You there were other times
    it's seemed
    You've left me
        way out
        in the dark
        alone
        to wait...
Until You became more important
than any answer
I was looking for.
            —Nancy Spiegelberg[1]

---

1. Nancy Spiegelberg and Dorothy Purdy, Fanfare: A Celebration of Belief (Portland, OR: Multnomah, 1981), p. 54.

Why We Wait

Reflect

When you seem to have no answer, there is always a reason-God uses these times to give you deep personal instruction, and it is not for anyone but you.

—Oswald Chambers

Have you had to wait for an answer to prayer?

How did you handle the wait?

Was it a time of learning for you? Were you able to get past the frustration and anger at God so you could come to Him with an attitude of submission and a desire to learn what He was trying to teach you?

Study

Read Hannah's story in 1 Samuel, chapters 1 and 2.

What does 1 Samuel 1:10-16 say about her emotions?

_____

_____

How does it describe her prayer?

_____

_____

Have you had similar prayers (times when you were desperate when you came to God)? What were they about?

_____

_____

One of the things that occurs when we wait is that we become *real* with God. When we come in desperation we lose our rote prayers based upon an immature view of God.

Deep honesty with God is a beginning point for spiritual maturity. We want to put on religious niceness and superficial fruits of the spirit; however, these will not last under the onslaught of tough circumstances. And that is what God wants. He wants a relationship with you based on honest emotions and real interaction.

Read David's prayer in Psalm 13:1-4. Have you ever felt like that?

_____

In Psalm 42:9-10, David prays a similar prayer. What is his attitude?

_____

Read Psalm 88. What are some of the actions David accuses God of?

_____

_____

Read Psalm 74:1 and Psalm 10:1. What did David say to God in these verses?

_____

_____

In Job 9:13-18, what does Job say about God?

_____

In Job 30:20-21?

_____

_____

These men, like us, had moments of real disappointment in God. At other moments, however, these same men showed tremendous faith and trust in God. The point is, they used their circumstances to deal with God. They didn't back away in silence when their prayers were unanswered. They came back again and expressed to God what they were feeling about those unanswered prayers. This opened the way for interaction with God, allowing God to reveal Himself, and it opened the door for new faith and maturity to grow in their hearts.

Receiving God's Grace

Where does Psalm 34:18 say God is when we are hurting?
_____

What does Psalm 62:8 and 142:1-2 instruct us to do?
_____
_____

What does Psalm 56:8 say about your tears?
_____

Psalm 6:8?
_____

Prayer of Response

In the space below, or in your journal, write out a prayer that reflects what you feel about your present circumstances, any unanswered prayers, or unfulfilled dreams.
_____
_____

Discussion

What does Psalm 40:1-3 say about waiting?

What happens in others' lives when we wait patiently? (verse 3b)

Can you share a time in your life when God made you wait and that waiting caused a change in you or in your desires?

CHAPTER 9

When God Says No

"Why did we even pray? What good did it do?" My son's questioning revealed his confusion and his sense of futility.

Some friends of ours, a young couple in our church, had just lost their baby. They had already been through several miscarriages, but with this pregnancy it looked like finally everything would work out. Then, in the fifth month, complications set in.

The church immediately began to pray that the wife could carry the baby to full term—but that didn't happen. The baby was born prematurely, weighing a little over one pound. With the miracles of modern medicine, however, the doctors still gave the baby a 50-50 chance. We were sure that with all the prayers she had a much better chance than that. The parents named her Faith and looked to God for a miracle.

Little Faith became the object of intercession for hundreds of people as everyone who heard about her began to pray. At one point, during a crisis that occurred on a Sunday, our pastor turned the evening service into a prayer meeting specifically for Faith. We interceded with tears and pleading, begging God to intervene.

She was so little; our hearts just ached for her to make it. Every ounce of weight she gained was cause for rejoicing. When her condition worsened and it became apparent that only a miracle could save her, the praying intensified, but after only nine days of life, she died.

In the days immediately following, God's grace was apparent in the lives of our young friends as they turned their faces to Him in acquiescence to His will. Their quiet and steady trust in God was a blessing to all of us. However, we were just finishing with dinner on the day of the funeral when our son's questioning began.

"Why pray?" Matt said at one point, "God just does what He wants anyway."

When we begin to talk to God, face-to-face, we come to know Him. However, the relationship we experience is a deep and complex one, and it won't always be easy for us. For as personal and intimate and loving as God will show Himself to be, there will be times when we come up against the hard, unchanging, and unyielding side of His nature. There will be times when God says no.

In those times when we're faced with the dreaded certainty that He is not going to do what we've asked Him to do, it can honestly seem like God "just does what He wants anyway." The loved one dies, the business ends in bankruptcy, the painful and tragic comes crashing into our lives. What happens then?

It's easy in those moments to feel that prayer is futile. Why pray? What good does it do?

But God isn't "doing what He wants anyway." He is doing what is best, for you and all involved.

When Jesus prayed in the garden the night before He was to die on the cross, He asked for "this cup to be taken away." God did not want His Son to go through that agony, and yet He said no, and He will sometimes say no to us.

There will be times when He will not be swayed by our tearful pleas for Him to deliver us from situations He intends for us to walk through completely. There will be times when His understanding will be hidden from us, and we will be forced to submit to harsh, bitter circumstances for which we can see no purpose. There will be times when He does not intervene, times when He is silent in answer to our supplications.

It is at this point in our relationship with God that we are forced to choose whether we truly believe in His goodness, in His love for us, and in His ability to bring good from everything that touches us.

It is at this point that we will again have a confrontation, a "dealing" with God. When we choose to come to Him in whatever state our emotions may be, then we can begin to receive new knowledge of Him. We will be given His grace, first of all, to get through the difficult days. We will be given His comfort, His love, and His assurance to sustain us as we walk through valleys with harsh shadows. And as we continue to come, He will impart new faith as He deepens our knowledge of Him.

When we choose to come to Him in spite of the no or the silence, His Spirit within us moves deeper, giving us a strong foundation of trust in our heavenly Father. Then He is free to begin to bring His miraculous good from what may have seemed too harsh to bear. After the children of Israel left Egypt and crossed the Red Sea, they were forced to travel three days without fresh water. They finally came to a place where there was water, but the water was bitter. They called the place "Marah," which means "bitterness."

The Israelites desperately cried out, "What are we to drink?" (Exodus 15:24). When Moses called out to God in their behalf, God told him to take a piece of wood and throw it into the water. When he did, the water became sweet.

God did not give the children of Israel new or different water to drink. Instead, He made the water they had sweet to their taste.

The wood that Moses threw into the water became a symbol of the cross of our Lord. Often the answers to our circumstances are not pleasing to us; in fact, they are hurtful and bitter and we cry out, "I don't like this, God! This can't be the water You want me to drink!" But the cross of Christ placed across our situation can make the bitter waters sweet.

God may not change the situation we have to face. Sometimes the answer is no, but He can make our circumstances bearable and ultimately sweet as He changes the bitterness of our attitude.

Often the circumstances we have walked through become treasures, like Goliath's armor, as we look back on them and say, "I'm glad God didn't change that situation because He used it to accomplish good in my life," or "It was difficult, but I'm so thankful for what God did through it."

C.I. Scofield wrote, "The bitter waters were in the very path of God's leading and stand for the trials of God's people, which are not for punishment but for education."

When we yield to God, bitter circumstances become the means by which God quenches the thirst of our spirit for more of Him as He fills us with Himself.

At first, we may not be able to experience that joy. We may have some difficult encounters with God until He is able to bring us to a place of acceptance and, ultimately, spiritual growth and maturity through the trials we may suffer.

Trials, pressures, problems, and even tragedies will ultimately bring good into our lives, but this can only happen when we continue to come to God, even in the midst of the anger, the hurt, the bewilderment, and the lack of any understanding about why something did or didn't happen.

> James 1:2-4 says:
>
> Consider it pure joy, my brothers, whenever you face trials of many kinds, because you know that the testing of your faith develops perseverance. Perseverance must finish its work so that you may be mature and complete, not lacking anything.

At some point in your relationship with God, your faith, your trust in Him, will be tested. It is inevitable, and it is your response during that test that will predict the outcome.

When you respond by turning away from God in anger, in hurt, or in silent withdrawal, you limit His access into your life and His ability to bring good from the circumstance. You also lose the most valuable opportunity you could have to know God in a closer, more intimate way.

James 1:2 is followed by the statement, "If any of you lacks wisdom, he should ask God" (v. 5). James is telling us it's okay to ask why. The important thing is that we go to God. That is our direction, during difficulties as well as any other time. "Come unto me." Going to God enables Him to impart His good to us.

He is always the answer, no matter what the situation is. He is always the answer whether we need deliverance, grace to keep going, help in trusting Him, or guidance about what to do. Whenever we are overwhelmed with adverse circumstances or hurtful situations, we can immediately fall on our knees before our heavenly Father and pour it all out.

There are times when we walk through dark shadows in circumstances that again and again pull us down into despair. During these times we will have to seek His face continually, leaning hard upon Him for help to get through the bewildering and frightening situations.

We may have to seek His face many times a day for strength to get through and grace to trust until our faith in Him grows stronger and we can more easily keep our eyes on Him. We may need to ask for His help to regain our trust in Him, pouring out all the fear and hurt, and waiting on Him to receive an assurance of His hand upon our lives. Every situation is different; sometimes He will immediately promise you deliverance, but when He doesn't, He will give you His assurance that He is with you and will use all for your good.

We can choose to hug our anger, hurt, or fear as long as we like; we can choose to look for help from other people or through a constant stream of activities; or we can choose to seek God's face until our hearts are again resting in Him.

In every encounter, as we submit, allowing His Spirit to freely flow through us, we will receive grace, help, nurturing, enabling, and, even when understanding is not given, we will receive peace.

Our knowledge of God will begin to grow deep roots, so that it permeates every part of our being, thus enabling the Holy Spirit of God access into the furthest reaches of our soul.

When turmoil strikes your life, you can be sure God has a gift of grace for you. It may be victory. He may deliver you and give you a miracle. But when He doesn't, when the answer is no, part of the good He wants to bring will be further knowledge of Himself, new growth for you, and deeper faith in His care and ever-present concern.

In our intimate journey of close relationship with God, forged in prayer, all of our encounters will not be pleasant—and yet God never allows anything to touch us unless He can bring good from it (Romans 8:28). As you come to Him, He can make the bitter waters sweet, He can impart to you His grace and help, and He can make Himself known to you.

Reflect

Until we come face to face with the deepest, darkest fact of life without damaging our view of God's character, we do not yet know Him.

—Oswald Chambers

Knowing God in dark days will mean wrestling with what we believe about Him. Are you going through a difficult time right now? Does it seem like God isn't helping?

How do you deal with God during dark days? Do you find it difficult to come to Him? Do you struggle with feeling that He is angry?

> distant?

> uncaring?

Study

Read Psalm 107.

This psalm gives brief sketches of different kinds of people: the lonely, the trapped, the afflicted, and the wanderers. Each is caught up in difficult circumstances and yet in each kind of circumstances God's hand is revealed. What is each group asked to do?

_____

_____

It is always God's goodness that comes into question when we are struggling with unanswered prayers. However, a foundation of belief in His goodness is built as we go through dealings because God has "good" for us in every circumstance we face. His character requires it and His Word promises it (Romans 8:28).

What does Nahum 1:7 say about the nature of God?

_____

What does Psalm 33:5 say the earth is full of?
_____

What does Psalm 52:1 say about the goodness of God?
_____

What does Psalm 34:8 instruct us to do?
_____

Receiving God's Goodness

It is imperative that our questions and struggles with unanswered prayers begin and end in the knowledge of God's goodness and love for us.

Look up and underline Isaiah 43:1-5. Write your name in place of Jacob and Israel.

Underline also Jeremiah 31:3, and write your name after the word "you."

Look up Psalm 42:8.

There will be times in your relationship with God that you will need to *choose* to believe in His goodness—no matter what circumstances say. Spend time in the Word, reaffirming the goodness of His character. Ask the Holy Spirit to help you get past your feelings about God, and choose to come to God and deal with Him.

Prayer of Response

In 2 Timothy 1:12, Paul makes a wonderful statement of belief. In light of whatever circumstances you are in today, will you make this statement?_____

Look up Psalm 42:11 also.

If you are experiencing difficult times (or even if you are not), pray one or both of these scriptures out loud. Do you mean it? No matter how you feel, pray in faith and ask the Holy Spirit to help you believe it.

Write out a personal prayer of trust and belief in God's goodness in the space below, or in your prayer journal.

_____

_____

_____

_____

Extra Help

Look up the following scriptures and write out some of the reasons God allows suffering:

Psalm 119:67 _____

Isaiah 52:4-6 (see first line of verse 6) _____

Hosea 5:15 _____

Romans 5:3-5 _____

2 Corinthians 1:3-5 _____

2 Corinthians 4:11-17 _____

Hebrews 12:5-11 _____

James 1:2-3 _____

1 Peter 1:6-8 _____

Discussion

Share some specific "no's" you feel God has said to you in the past. What good did God bring from those times?

CHAPTER 10

Cleaning Time

I was angry with Jula. Her room was a mess. Of course it probably wasn't any worse than most teenagers' rooms, but it irritated me that day. There were people coming over. Also, she was running late, and consequently, I had to rearrange my time schedule.

I complained about one thing after another, treating her to more than one parental sermon. Then I took her to school, drove home, and got down to pray.

I hadn't said two words before I sensed the Lord's interruption. "I don't treat you like that."

Immediately I was very quiet; God doesn't usually speak to my heart that abruptly. He began to remind me what a good daughter I had and how pleased He was with her and how displeased He was with me for my treatment of her that morning.

Then He started to probe a little deeper, revealing to me why I had treated her like that. It wasn't that she had really done anything wrong. She just had not fit in with my plans for the day, and had caused me to have to change some things I had wanted to do that morning in order to help her. I had punished her for it, too, with my severe tongue.

There was no arguing as God opened my eyes to my own sinfulness. As I realized how ultimately selfish my anger had been, I asked for God's forgiveness, knowing I would also need to ask for Jula's.

As we begin to come to God consistently, spending time with Him and allowing Him into our lives in greater measure, we will begin to come upon areas of our lives that need to be exposed and changed.

Time in God's presence will always begin to reveal what is really in our hearts.

When we deal with God, coming to Him regularly with everything that is happening to us, we give Him the opportunity to work with us. When we come to Him and relate how bad this or that situation is and how we hate it, we are giving Him the opportunity to use that situation to teach us—perhaps to reveal to us why we got into the mess and what it is in us that brought us to that point. As I mentioned earlier, this is sometimes the very reason people don't want to spend too much time with God: they are afraid of exposure.

Recently our company received new personnel tests for our employees. The tests were to help diagnose people's strengths and weaknesses so we could all do a better job. The employees, however, were not at all thrilled about taking the test. Everyone was on the defensive. "Why do I have to do this?" "What are you looking for?" One person said, "I already know my strengths, and I don't want to hear about my weaknesses."

That last comment really sums up our feelings, doesn't it? None of us wants to hear about our weaknesses. We naturally shy away from too much exposure or too much probing if it means confronting faults.

Exposure is hard on us. We don't want to face shortcomings because we mistakenly base our identity upon whatever we have decided through the years gives us our value. Too much exposure of our weaknesses may quickly smash that fragile hold on our sense of identity. Subconsciously, we may decide that if we never deal with God this can't happen and we can keep feeling good about ourselves.

It's a sad misconception, which robs from us true insight into ourselves, God, and our true worth. You and I, lovingly created in the image of God, have inherit value and worth, but our sin heritage has left us with distorted thinking. Even after coming to Christ, many of us keep using our old value system, which bases our worth upon our "goodness."

This works against us whether the image we have of ourselves is good, or bad. If we feel worthy because we see ourselves as basically good, we will view any probing as unnecessary. Consequently, we will have difficulty coming to know that our true value to God lies in who we are in Christ, not in how "good" we might be.

If our self-image is already faulty, we may feel we can't deal with any more faultfinding. It's rejection to us, and we don't think we can handle it.

For some people, correction is difficult because they are so busy chastising themselves that real repentance is unknown to them. Repentance is just one more cord on the powerful whip with which they already flog themselves. This kind of ineffectual self-effort has to be lain aside so that the true work of the Holy Spirit can begin in our lives.

True repentance brings a fresh awareness of who we are in Christ, a new awareness of the immensity of God's grace and love, and a feeling of peace that our sin has been dealt with, forgiven, cast aside, and forgotten. It is not the condemnation and heavy burden of guilt that some people choose to hug to themselves.

God never condemns us. He is only interested in delivering us from the power of our carnal nature and the havoc it plays in our lives as it alienates us from Him. When we don't have the opportunity to see what is hidden deep in our hearts, we never really understand what repentance is.

Repentance carries a "sackcloth" connotation that is repugnant to us. We picture self-flagellation and degradation. The deep root of pride, present in each of us, makes repentance seem demeaning and painful. We avoid it like the plague.

At the same time, true repentance involves a kind of glaring honesty that we may not think we're ready for. Or it may be something for which we don't think we have a need. So often we do not see our sin for what it is. We offer God excuses for our sins, instead of repentance:

"I inherited this tendency from my grandfather."
"I've always had a temper."
"I'm this way because of my lousy childhood."
"All men have a problem with lust."

The way we look at sin will always be at variance with the way God views it, until we come into true repentance. Repentance is submission in its purest form. It is taking our powerful "self-life" and bringing it to

God for His destruction. Submitting to God isn't going to destroy our personality (we often mistakenly think that), but it will put an ax to the root of self that constantly raises its will against God's.

Repentance is a process that begins at salvation and continues throughout our life. Only as we actively participate in this process will God be allowed full access into our lives, and only then can a close relationship develop.

And so the process begins...

> Have mercy on me, O God, according to your unfailing love; according to your great compassion blot out my transgressions. Wash away all my iniquity and cleanse me from my sin.
> —Psalm 51:1-2

I decided one day to add another job to my teenagers' chores: cleaning their bathroom. My reasoning for many of the things I ask them to do is as much for their training as anything else, and this was something I felt they should learn to do right.

When I visit them after they are grown and living on their own, I do not want to have to clean while I am there. I've heard horror stories from other mothers about how their kids live at college. So while I had a few more years with them at home, I intended to put some extra effort into training them.

After I broke the news that from now on they would be responsible for cleaning their bathroom, I showed them how to do the job properly. I got out the cleansers, sponges, and brushes, and talked about the need for disinfectants, scrubbing, and cleanliness. I demonstrated all my cleaning techniques and then stood guard over them the first few times, watching to make sure they did it right, all the while giving out little homilies like "a job worth doing is worth doing well."

I wish I could say that from that point on their bathroom was spotless, but the truth of the matter is there was a constant war between us about the way they did the job, and the way I thought it should be done. One of their bathrooms was also the guest bath and, if for no other reason, I expected it to be cleaned the way I had shown them. I was forever calling them back to say, "Does this look clean to you?" "Did you even bother to wipe the counter?" or "Just look at that! Did you even touch it?" And I routinely heard comments such as:

"Who cares?"
"It doesn't hurt it to be dirty."
"Nobody ever looks at that."
"It's good enough!"

One day, when I called Jula back and pointed at the sink fixtures because it was obvious she hadn't touched them (there was a pink grime around the base of each one), she said, "That doesn't come off."

"Yes, it does, Jula," I countered, "but you have to actually put the cleanser on it and then scrub a little. It won't come off by just pouring some water over it." She groaned and took the sponge from me. I heard her muttering as I walked out of the room. It sounded to me like she said, "as if anyone cares."

My children's typical reaction to cleaning the bathroom is just like our reaction to God when He wants to clean us up.

"It's not so bad. So and so is much worse."
"Is this really necessary?"
"No one sees that."

We never think we're dirty enough to warrant such heavy-duty scrubbing—and we never like it!

Everything in us screams, "Cleaning time again? You just dealt with something two years ago, God. Is it really necessary again, so soon?"

It's always easier to let things go. To ignore the scum around the edges and to hope that no one else notices, either.

But God isn't willing to do that. Sometimes when we come to Him in prayer and are asking for something important to us, or questioning why something isn't going the way we would like, God will begin to point out the pink scum around the edge.

So often sin is the real cause of the problems we are in, and sometimes it's right in the way of our receiving what we want from God. Psalm 66:18 says, "If I regard iniquity in my heart, the Lord will not hear me" (KJV). God's close-up scrutiny can be hurtful. We feel threatened, and our reaction can go any of several ways:

We can refuse to allow God to confront the sin, turning a deaf ear to His promptings and pushing Him away so we can have a more distant relationship—one that doesn't require total openness.

We can accept His dealings and begin the work of repentance. We can learn what true repentance is.

Or we can do a kind of half-job with sin and repentance—the same kind of half-job my children do when they clean their bathroom.

A friend showed me a letter from a pastor who had spent the weekend in their home. The pastor had taken the time to write and give counsel about a problem he saw going on in the home and how it all related back to my friend. It was a thoughtful, kind letter, obviously written out of a heart of love and concern.

When I finished reading the letter, I handed it back without saying anything, wondering how my friend had received the counsel. He smiled wryly and said, "You know, he's right on. My actions are not only affecting that member of the family, but all of them."

We talked about it for a few minutes. I was impressed by his willingness to accept the criticism so lovingly given. As we ended the conversation and my friend walked away, I thought about what had been said. He had been ready to admit there was a problem, and he was thankful that his friend had cared enough to point it out. It was obvious he wanted to change. But then I remembered a similar conversation we'd had six or seven months before when my friend had been confronted by his wife about the same problem. He had been open and honest about it then, too.

I wondered if it would ever go any further than that. So often, it doesn't. Admitting the problem and feeling sorry about it, and perhaps discussing the need for change with others, sometimes acts as a catharsis for us. We feel good about the self-revelation process and look at it as growth.

We can see our problems and our need for change. Sometimes we can even be very upfront about character flaws. "Oh yes, I do have a temper." "Yeah, I've always had a problem with lust." But often our admission is more like acceptance. "That's the way I am. It's too bad, but..." We may even pray about it, but often we just pray about the consequences, the problems, or the outward manifestations of our sin, and we fail to ever really deal with God about the root causes.

It is possible to offer words of confession but still fail to repent. There are some good examples of this in the Bible.

In Exodus 9:27, Pharaoh said, "I have sinned," when the plague of hail came across his land—but his words changed when the circumstances changed, and again his heart was hardened.

In 1 Samuel 15:24, Saul said, "I have sinned," when Samuel confronted him with his blatant disobedience to God's word—but his very next words were excuses and a request that Samuel still honor him.

In both instances, the confession of sin was a confession only to man and not a confrontation with God, who alone could forgive and atone for his sins. Why was this?

Neither man was willing to come fully into submission to God and be changed. When we settle for this kind of "confession," we will continue living with the problems and sorrows that our sins cause.

Repentance is seeing sin as God sees it, with grief over the sin and an overwhelming desire for change. Until our awareness of our sin develops in us the kind of godly sorrow that Paul speaks about, we have not come into true repentance:

> See what this godly sorrow has produced in you: what earnestness, what eagerness to clear yourselves, what indignation, what alarm, what longing, what concern, what readiness to see justice done.
> —2 Corinthians 7:11

Until we experience anguish over our sinfulness and inability to change and, in desperation, cast ourselves at the feet of Jesus, we are not going to experience truly lasting effects from our moments of self-awareness and honesty.

Remorse and acknowledgment of sin are not enough. Mankind is not going to change until he sees how deeply the roots of sin go into his life and how far-reaching its effects are. And until his despair and cry for help reach crisis proportions, he is not yet aware of how totally helpless he is to help himself, and how totally dependent he must be upon Jesus to save him from his own sinfulness.

At this point, God can act to bring about real change. This is what godly sorrow is. It is recognizing the depth of our sinfulness and being overwhelmed by it enough to cry out in desperation to God for forgiveness and help:

> For I know my transgressions, and my sin is always before me. Against you, you only, have I sinned and done what is evil in your sight, so that you are proved right when you speak and justified when you judge.
> —Psalm 51:3-4

Reflect

The paradox for most Christians is that we know and admit we're sinners in the broad sense of needing a Savior, but we shy away from specifics. We know we're self-involved, demanding, or critical in a general sense, but we would rather not deal with the specifics of it.

What has been your most common response to the sin in your own life? Do you…

Ignore it?

Justify it?

Minimize it?

Feel sorry for awhile and then forget about it?

Confess it?

What sin have you confessed before that, if you are really honest, is still a problem for you?

Cleaning Time

Study

How does Psalm 38:17-18 describe David's reaction to his own sin?

What reaction to sin does Lamentations 1:20 describe?

Have you ever experienced that kind of feeling about your sin?

What emotion does Paul talk about in 2 Corinthians 7:9-10?

According to 2 Corinthians 7:11, what does godly sorrow produce?

Have you ever had this happen to you?

According to Hosea 14:1-2 and Psalm 32:5, what should always be our first step?

In 1 John 1:9 and Isaiah 43:25, what does God promise to do about our sin?

Receiving God's Forgiveness

Have you been tolerating sin in your life?

What sin(s) have you been excusing or justifying?
_____

What is it you need to specifically call sin?
_____

Pray Psalm 51 this week. Paraphrase some of the scriptures in your journal. Personalize it and be specific.

If you don't already, make confession a part of your prayer time each day. Prayerfully consider your last 24 hours and ask for forgiveness for any actions that were ungodly, unkind, thoughtless, mean, impatient, and untruthful. Ask God to forgive you for impure thoughts, selfishness, self-centeredness, and wrong motives. Be specific. You might also need to confess your tendency to wallow in self-pity, to hold on to bitterness, or to allow anxiety to rule your life.

Discussion

What do you think is the difference between godly sorrow and condemnation?

Some people struggle with condemnation and guilt that have nothing to do with God's dealing with sin in their lives. When God talks to you, He will be *specific* about your sin. Vague feelings of condemnation are never from God.

> *A person will easily say, "Oh yes, I know I am a sinner," but when he comes into the presence of God he cannot get away with such a broad and indefinite statement. Our conviction is focused on our specific sin, and we realize...what we really are. This is always the sign that a person is in the presence of God. There is never any vague sense of sin, but a focusing on the concentration of sin in some specific, personal area of life.*
> —Oswald Chambers

CHAPTER 11

Repentance: Grief and Joy

Even when we are willing to repent and deal with our overt sins or our more obvious sin tendencies, we may still be very reluctant to allow the Holy Spirit to probe very deeply into the root sins that stem from the strong "self" in all of us. As we grow in our relationship with Christ, these root sins will become more apparent. Once recognized, they must be brought to the cross so that the work of God's Spirit will not be hindered in our lives.

But the process can involve some scrubbing!

A few years ago, when I was Women's Ministries' director at our church, I was busy planning our annual women's retreat. We had already arranged for the main speaker, but I was still trying to put together several short seminars. One of my friends had a brother who taught courses in communications at a college and at business seminars, and through her we hoped to get him to come for a session at our retreat.

The subject was an interesting one, and I knew its inclusion in our schedule would give an added sophistication to our conference, so I began to pursue it. I had a hard time reaching the speaker although my friend had already asked him to come. As I went through several weeks of trying to get in touch with him to finalize the date and time, there was a nagging thought in the back of my mind, "You'd better pray about this."

However, I had been praying about the retreat for months, and surely the idea for this had been born out of those prayers. As the weeks went by, I began to feel a little frustrated, since I wanted to take care of all the details. I began to pray a little more about it. Each time I prayed, however, there was a distinct silence.

It was soon time to print the brochures, so I stepped up my pursuit. One morning I was finally able to talk to the speaker's secretary and leave a message that I would call back several hours later. After the call I couldn't seem to ignore the inner nagging, so I went to my room to pray. As I prayed I began to verbalize to God how badly I wanted this speaker. "The women will enjoy it. The subject is needed and relevant. Please, take care of the details, Lord."

As I prayed I felt the disquiet again, and I began to argue with God. "God, I can't believe You don't want us to have this speaker. You know how much we, as wives and mothers, need to grow in our communication skills, and this is just the kind of thing that will be appealing on the brochure. We want this retreat to be well attended."

On and on I struggled, expressing my feelings to God until out of my mouth came the words, "God, I want this speaker, and I am going to call him, and I don't know how You can stop me!"

Then I sat there for a moment, stunned. Had that really come from my mouth? I could hardly believe I had spoken those words. Where had they come from?

As the realization of exactly where those words came from slowly sank in, I began to cry. Suddenly, I was face-to-face with my own willfulness.

Shock mingled with disbelief as I tried to come to grips with this new revelation. Even though I had been confronted with major root sins in my life before, submission was one area in which I felt I did not have a problem. All my life I had been submissive to God, choosing to serve Him from an early age and endeavoring throughout my life to follow His path.

I had been strong-willed with other people, but never with God—or so I thought. Now I could see beneath the layers of apparent submission to a whole other self, and it was not a pretty sight:

> Surely I have been a sinner from birth, sinful from the time my mother conceived me.
>
> —Psalm 51:5

Though I felt I had never had a problem submitting to God, it now became apparent that I had never really been put in the position of coming up against Him in something I wanted and He didn't. Frankly,

Repentance: Grief and Joy

there had been little up to this point to have a confrontation about. I was raised in a Christian home and had accepted Christ as a young child. I continued to serve Him through my teen years, married a Christian man, and had lived a life relatively free of rebellion. God had directed my path with gentle maneuverings and guided my footsteps because of the prayers of my parents and my own choices. I did have a heart after God, but now I saw that something else was also there:

> Surely you desire truth in the inner parts; you teach me wisdom in the inmost place.
> —Psalm 51:6

I began to grieve over my sinfulness, over the root of self-will that was now so apparent. For the next few days I felt sorrow, along with a sense of frailty. I had been stripped bare of yet another layer of my own "goodness," and I turned to God with words of sorrow and repentance as I came to grips with this new understanding of my sinful nature:

> Cleanse me with hyssop, and I will be clean; wash me, and I will be whiter than snow.
> —Psalm 51:7

The result was God's grace and love flowing toward me in increasing measure as He began to pour Himself into the empty "root area" that had been pulled up and needed to be filled with Him. God lovingly bathed me in Himself, reassuring me over and over of His love. Soon the sorrow was replaced with an incredible feeling of lightness and joy:

> Let me hear joy and gladness; let the bones you have crushed rejoice.
> —Psalm 51:8

When God chooses to deal with root sins, we are going to experience some times of real sorrow for our sinfulness. We will become agonizingly aware of how deeply our motives and our reactions to people and situations are rooted in the sins of pride, self-will, self-centeredness, selfishness, and a desire for approval.

But God's grace will also be extended to give us greater certainty that, even though "in me dwelleth no good thing" (Romans 7:18 KJV), yet in Him we find "everything we need for life and godliness" (2 Peter 1:3).

True repentance does involve grief over our sin, but interestingly enough, the effect of this emotional storm is incredible freedom. The burden of having to pretend is gone. Not only is the weight of sin lifted, so is another layer of self-delusion. John 8:32 says, "You will know the truth, and the truth will set you free."

In place of delusion is the much deeper knowledge of your incredible value to God. Your worth is seen in a new light: in truth instead of illusion. You are valuable, but not because of your "goodness." Your value is that you were created in God's express image and endowed with a personality, capabilities, and talents that delight your creator.

This kind of interaction with God brings a deeper understanding of yourself and your relationship with Him. A foundation of knowledge about God is formed, giving you a sense of eternal things and your unique place in them.

There is one other gift that comes from a time of true repentance: a fresh and vibrant love for Christ. This principle is revealed clearly in a story from one of the Gospels:

> Now one of the Pharisees invited Jesus to have dinner with him, so he went to the Pharisee's house and reclined at the table. When a woman who had lived a sinful life in that town learned that Jesus was eating at the Pharisee's house, she brought an alabaster jar of perfume, and as she stood behind him at his feet weeping, she began to wet his feet with her tears. Then she wiped them with her hair, kissed them and poured perfume on them.
>
> When the Pharisee who had invited him saw this, he said to himself, "If this man were a prophet, he would know who is touching him and what kind of woman she is—that she is a sinner."
>
> —Luke 7:36-39

Repentance: Grief and Joy

Then Jesus related a parable of two men who owed money to a moneylender. One owed a large sum, the other just a small amount, but neither could repay the money. The moneylender canceled the debts of each man.

Jesus asked the Pharisee, "Now which of them will love him more?"

Simon the Pharisee answered, "I suppose the one who had the bigger debt canceled."

Jesus replied, "You have judged correctly." Then he went on to describe the difference in treatment He had received from Simon and the sinful woman still weeping at His feet:

> I came into your house. You did not give me any water for my feet [a common and very minimal gesture of hospitality], but she wet my feet with her tears and wiped them with her hair. You did not give me a kiss [another common form of greeting], but this woman, from the time I entered, has not stopped kissing my feet. You did not put oil on my head, but she has poured perfume on my feet. Therefore, I tell you, her many sins have been forgiven—for she loved much. But he who has been forgiven little loves little.
>
> —Luke 7:44-47

This section of Scripture could, at first glance, be interpreted to mean that people with very sinful lives will have more of a love for Jesus than those who receive Him as children or those without a background of terrible sin. But that isn't what Jesus is saying.

"He who has been forgiven little loves little."

It isn't the kind of sins we've committed, or the amount of sinning we have done. It is the quality of our repentance that Jesus alludes to here. It is not the magnitude of our sins that determines the love you and I will have for a forgiving God and a sin-atoning Christ. It is the amount of forgiveness we have asked for and received. It isn't the sins. It is the forgiveness, and in this we are all in the same boat.

We are all in need of forgiveness, much forgiveness. The root of self that is the catalyst behind all sin is the same for everyone. When you look past the outward acts of sin to the inside of man, the heart is the same for all. The need for repentance is the same. Simon the Pharisee had as much need for repentance as the sinful woman. His heart was as black as hers.

Sin in the person raised in an abusive environment will take a different form than that of someone loved and raised with a strong sense of identity. But the root of self is still the same, whether manifested by inappropriate social behavior or by manipulating the people around us with our charm, whether by forcing others to do what we want with a gun, or forcing them through the strength of our will or our position of authority.

It is not the outward manifestation of these roots of sin that will make the difference in our love for Christ. It is the "degree of our repentance" that is the gauge upon which our love for God can be measured.

When we begin to allow the light of Christ to shine upon those hidden areas, when we begin to look at sin in the same way God does, and when we begin to experience godly sorrow over it, then we will begin to experience a love for God unlike anything we've ever known.

We see ourselves and we despair, but at the same time His grace and love flow toward us. We see Him in a new light, and we are overcome with gratitude and love at His willingness to forgive us, to love us, and to want a relationship with us. In those moments of deep sorrow and repentance, God will reach down in tenderness and mercy to bathe us in His love and forgiveness.

Understanding what repentance is, and beginning to experience the reality of it in our dealings with Him will enable us to come into a completely different realm in our relationship with God. For until we really comprehend how desperately and completely we need to be forgiven, we will never fully appreciate the depth of Jesus' love for us, and we will never be able to love and appreciate Him as He is worthy to be loved.

> You do not delight in sacrifice, or I would bring it; you do not take pleasure in burnt offerings. The sacrifices of God are a broken spirit; a broken and contrite heart, O God, you will not despise.
> —Psalm 51:16-17

Repentance: Grief and Joy

Reflect

Just as I was unaware of what was in my heart (willfulness) until God used my circumstances to reveal it, there may be things in your heart of which you are unaware because you haven't experienced the kinds of circumstances that reveal them. From time to time through different situations, God will bring things to light for which we are in need of a deeper work of cleansing. In these moments, God deals with the underlying attitudes of our hearts.

Study

What do Proverbs 16:2 and 21:2 say about our perception of ourselves?

_____

What does Jeremiah 17:9 say about the heart of man?_____

What "rhetorical question" is asked?_____

Psalm 19:12 asks a similar question. What is it?_____

What does Proverbs 30:12 say about people who feel they are okay?

_____

In light of these scriptures, do you still feel you know your own heart?

_____

Using the following scriptures, list the things that God sees and knows.

Job 34:21_____

Psalm 44:21_____

Ezekiel 11:5_____

1 Chronicles 28:9_____

Learning to Pray

Psalm 90:8_____

Have you ever had a time when God revealed something in you that you didn't know was there? Or perhaps didn't think of as sin? When God's probing reveals a root sin, usually it isn't something we have never thought of. However, we haven't thought of it as sin; it's just who we are!

What is David's request in Psalm 26:2? _____

In Job 13:23, what does Job ask God to do? _____

Do you see the necessity for this request?_____

How does David describe the effects of this kind of dealing in Psalm 38:1-10 (notice verse 8) and in Psalm 51 (notice verses 8 and 17)?

_____

What does Psalm 34:18 say is God's response to the brokenhearted and crushed in spirit?

_____

Receiving God's Examining

Read Psalm 139 and prayerfully consider the last two scriptures. Ask God to show you if you have ignored His dealings in the past. Tell Him you are willing to see whatever He wants to show you.

Another phrase used to describe this process is "dying to self." Do you understand how "self" is at the root of all sin?

It is "self" we are accommodating whenever we are…

> controlling
> judgmental
> angry
> self-pitying

        resentful
            stubborn
willful
    proud
        overly concerned with what people think
heedless
    impatient
        manipulative
self-involved
    selfish
        demanding of God and other people
self-righteous
    critical
        blaming.

Prayerfully consider this list, asking God to examine your heart. Is there an area about which He has been trying to deal with you?

Ask God to allow you to see the sin as He sees it, and to show you how deeply the roots of it go. Insight into root sins will reveal a great deal to us about ourselves and our relationships, clearing up misconceptions and revealing our part in the problem we may be having with someone.

Discussion

If you feel you want to, share with your group a sin that God has been dealing with you about. See James 5:16.

Pray for one another.

CHAPTER 12

Trading Rocks for Jewels

One year on a family vacation, we stayed in a hotel that was right on the beach. Our room overlooked the ocean, and we could sit on the balcony and watch the tides come in and out. We fell asleep each night with the sound of waves crashing.

It was a wonderful time. The kids were at such a great age. Matt was ten and Jula eight and everything to them was an adventure. We often watched them from the room as they played with other kids, going through an assortment of activities. One day while we were watching them, they began to systematically pick things up from the sand. We wondered what they were doing; they seemed so industrious.

When they finally came back to the room we found out. They had brought with them a collection of rocks—but you would have thought they had found gold. Each of them went through their individual array, showing us each rock and saying, "Look at this one!"

"This is the best!"
"See how this shines."
"This is my very favorite."

Chuck and I dutifully looked at each one, oohing and aahing, even though there was nothing noticeably special about any of their "treasures."

Jula and Matt made a special place for the rocks and carefully guarded them, planning to save them and take them home as souvenirs.

A few hours later, Chuck was standing on the balcony looking down at the beach. He happened to notice three large garbage cans placed directly below our room, which was on the fifth floor.

"Matt, can I have one of your rocks?"

Matthew looked up from the game he and Jula were playing. "Why, Dad?"

"I want to see if I can hit that garbage can down there."

Matt hurried over to stand next to his dad and look down at the beach. He looked back up at Chuck, and I saw the same gleam in his eye that his dad already had. He rushed back into the room to get a rock.

I watched to see which of his precious treasures he would give up, but he didn't even take time to decide. He just grabbed one and ran back out to the balcony.

By this time Jula was out there too. I followed, and in a matter of seconds we had a game going: "Who Can Put a Rock in the Garbage Can."

Can you guess where we got the rocks?

It was amazing how little value the rocks had then to the kids. They didn't even remember that they had planned to keep them.

Nobody gave a moment's thought to trying to save them. After all…they were just rocks.

When we begin to come to God in relational prayer, one of the most obvious benefits we receive is the light of Christ shining truth upon a lot of the rocks we've been treasuring. As we gradually learn to bring to Him our thoughts and the happenings of our life, He can begin to focus His light upon our tightly-held misbeliefs and distorted thought processes. This will begin to make a difference in many areas, beginning with the way we think.

So much of our thinking, even as Christians, is distorted by the sin heritage with which we were born. Centuries of living apart from the Spirit of God have wreaked havoc with mankind's perceptions, reasoning, and beliefs. Our heavenly Father must begin at salvation to bring illumination and correction.

It is a lengthy process and involves every aspect of our life. Many basic principles that apply to our natural, physical life, such as making decisions based on circumstances, or placing value on position or success, do not apply to life in the Spirit. We must learn to submit our thoughts to God so that His light can bring understanding and correction:

> Now we have received, not the spirit of the world, but the Spirit who is from God, that we might know the things that have been freely given to us by God. These things we also speak, not in words which man's wisdom teaches but which the Holy Spirit teaches, comparing spiritual things with spiritual.
> —1 Corinthians 2:12,13 NKJV

We often want to bring our own rationale and logic into looking at matters in our Christian life. We say, in effect, "I'll decide what's best, based on my knowledge and understanding of the facts...and You just take care of it, Lord."

Although God gave us a mind with which to think and reason, He never intended it to be the source of our decisions. He intended for us to be guided by His Spirit within us.

When we come to God, we have spent years living with our own soulish intellect in control. Gradually God must begin to reveal to us how faulty our reasoning can be, and it may not be an easy process. We will stubbornly cling to our rocks: our confidence in our own intellectual abilities, our insistence that we always will know what needs to be done in life's situations, and the tendency for our decisions to be motivated by carnal interests and desires.

In Mark 8:31, Jesus began to tell the disciples about the things that He must suffer. He said He would be rejected by the elders and killed. Then after three days He would rise again. The passage continues: "He spoke plainly about this, and Peter took him aside and began to rebuke him" (v. 32).

But when Jesus turned and looked at the disciples, He rebuked Peter. "Out of my sight, Satan!" He said. "You do not have in mind the things of God, but the things of men" (v. 33).

He then told them that if anyone wanted to come after him, he must *deny himself* and take up his cross and follow.

Peter's way of thinking was very natural, an automatic reaction to Christ's words of suffering, and yet Jesus rebuked him severely. He had to get across to the disciples and to us that we must not try to superimpose our own reactions to events upon God. Our natural responses and thinking will not be the way He responds or reasons, and we cannot try to dictate His thinking. Instead we must learn how He thinks and join Him in throwing away some of the rocks we have been saving for years.

In relational prayer we will become more aware of our need to have His wisdom continually flowing through us, and we will desire to know His thoughts on matters more and more. We will stop trusting "our own understanding" and begin to cry out for God's:

> Trust in the Lord with all your heart, and *lean not on your own understanding*; in all your ways acknowledge Him, and He shall direct your paths.
> —Proverbs 3:5-6 NKJV, emphasis added

Our thinking must gradually be altered as we discover God's principles and learn to know God Himself through His Word and through dealing with Him in prayer. As we go through experiences with Him, coming to Him in prayer for His insight and His understanding, we will gradually begin to see as He sees and learn to stop leaning on our own understanding.

Paul says, "Let this mind be in you which was also in Christ Jesus" (Philippians 2:5 NKJV). It will be necessary to choose over and over to submit ourselves, our mind, and our thoughts to God.

> Show me your ways, O Lord, teach me your paths; guide me in your truth and teach me.
> —Psalm 25:4-5

Reflect

We spend our lives worrying about what other people think, striving for the world's idea of success, and trusting in our own abilities. When you add in all the distortions and misbeliefs that we pick up from dysfunctional parenting, the constant bombardment from a sinful culture, and the lies and deceptions that Satan throws our way, it's easy to see why our "understanding" can be mixed up.

Nothing in our Christian life will bring as much correction to our thought lives as time spent in God's presence and in His Word. Are you aware of your need in this area? Have you spent enough time with God, in His Word and in His presence, so that you are becoming aware of the difference between His ways and yours?

Have any of your ways of thinking and reacting been exposed for the "rocks" they really are?

What kind of "rocks" have influenced your behavior in the past?

You may already be aware of some thinking patterns that are destructive in your life: worry, obsessive thoughts, negativity, self-pity, lustful or impure thoughts. But there are also more subtle thinking patterns that will take time and growth in your relationship with God before they are exposed for the rocks they are: distortions of truth about God, prideful thinking, belief systems based on faulty reasoning.

It is important to begin a process of examining our beliefs and thought processes under the guidance of the Holy Spirit, endeavoring to align our thoughts with God's way of thinking, and seeking to build our spiritual walk so that our thought processes are more reflective of the Spirit of Christ that lives in us. We need to begin to see the carnality that is at the root of so much of our thinking by allowing God to begin His process of exposing our thinking patterns to the light of Christ within us.

Study

What does Isaiah 55:8-9 say about God's thoughts and ours?

_____

What does Proverbs 14:12 say about the thoughts (ways) of man?

_____

What are we instructed to do in Proverbs 3:5?

_____

Letting go of our understanding takes time, and the process involves learning to know God's ways.

According to Romans 12:1-2, what needs to happen to our mind?
_____

According to the following scriptures, what actions are involved in the process?

Lamentations 3:40 _____

Psalm 25:4-5 _____

Proverbs 23:12 _____

Psalm 119:11, 130 _____

2 Corinthians 10:5 _____

John 7:17 _____

Philippians 4:8 _____

How does God help us (John 16:13 and 15)? _____

Look back over the list. What actions are you already taking?
_____

Receiving God's Thoughts

Pray the following prayer or something like it today.

> Dear Father,
>
> Please help me to exchange my way of thinking for Yours. I want to think the way you do, to act the way you would act, and to react to situations as You would. Show me "rocks" that have been a part of my thinking process.

Let my thoughts reflect Your thoughts, my words reflect Your words, and my actions reflect You and Your character. I submit my life to You today.

Amen.

Discussion

Share some of the ways God has been changing your thinking.

Pray for one another in the area of your thought lives. Use one of the scriptures in the Scripture Study section as a basis for prayer.

Something More

Since many people struggle in the area of their thought life, I want to give you some prayers that may be of help to you. Consider making one of the following sentence prayers a way of life for you:

"Lord, bring my thoughts into line with Your truth today!"

"Lord, help my thoughts to reflect Your thoughts"

"Guard my thoughts today, Lord."

"Jesus, let Your thoughts be in me today."

Second Corinthians 10:4-5 can be invaluable to you if you need help in this area. I have used it as a prayer countless times when praying for myself and for others.

Meditate on the promise in verse 4 regarding God's power over our thought life and begin to verbalize the words as part of your prayer life.

Memorize: Philippians 4:8 and 2 Corinthians 10:4-5.

CHAPTER 13

What Does God Sound Like?

I think of those rocks sometimes when someone says, "God told me...."

People want to believe they hear God's voice, and yet so often those of us around them silently question the source of their "voice." Often when someone says, "God told me to do such and such," and it doesn't work out, they either blame God or blithely go on to something else God "tells" them without ever dealing with the fact that they may not have heard from God the first time.

From big-name media personalities to the new Christian in our Bible study, we all struggle when faced with the realization that not everything we thought God told us was spoken by Him.

God does tell us things, but it is amazing how many of the things "God said" turn out to be "rocks."

And really that's okay—if the person trying to pass off "rocks" as precious jewels will slowly begin to learn the difference. The problem comes when someone continues saving "rocks" year after year instead of seeking to know the true voice of God.

But what does God's voice sound like? How do we know when He is speaking to us? Is every good thought from God? How about every spiritual one?

Starting a rescue mission in San Francisco is a good thought, even a spiritual one. There is a need. But is it God telling us all to go start a rescue mission?

What about our ego that wants to do something "spiritual" or great for God? Could that be the source of the voices we're hearing? Or perhaps it's a sense of guilt over all we have or a need to try and earn our salvation. How do we know? How do we find discernment? How do we learn to know God's voice? How do we learn to tell the difference between God's voice and the other voices that clamor for our attention?

Bruce Olson, in a November 1989 issue of Charisma magazine, relates a story of an incident that happened to him during his first years as a missionary to the Motilone tribe in Colombia. He had gone out into the jungle with a hunting party, and as they walked through the dense forest the birds and monkeys began their chattering reaction to the intrusion.

On that day, however, the noise seemed to get louder and louder as millions of katydids joined in the squawking and screeching. The noise level was so high that their human voices were nearly drowned out. Bruce was astonished at the volume of sound.

He turned to the person walking nearby and shouted, "Listen to that! Isn't it incredible?"

The Indian nodded his agreement and shouted back, "Yes. We heard it too. It's a piping turkey!"

Bruce was shocked at the answer. A piping turkey? All he had heard was chaotic, ear-shattering noise! How could anyone notice the voice of one lone turkey in the midst of that racket?

The Motilone saw his confusion and signaled him to stop and listen. When he did, it took him several minutes to pick out which sounds were which—animals, birds, insects, humans. Then, slowly, the separate voices became distinguishable.

Finally, after more patient listening, he heard it. Behind the hue and cry of the jungle, behind the voices of his companions, behind the quiet sound of his own breathing, was the haunting, reedy voice of the piping turkey.

It was a poignant moment because suddenly Bruce wondered what else he was missing, not only in the jungles, but in his own spiritual life. How much had he overlooked because he failed to patiently tune in to God's subtle voice in the midst of life's clamor and activity?

We have the same kind of hearing problems. We so often miss what God has to say to us because we are so busy listening to everyone and everything else, whether it's the advice of friends to whom we run when in trouble or the screaming of our own emotions and desires that try to dictate our responses to life's situations.

What Does God Sound Like?

God's voice is quiet and can easily be missed. It takes patience, desire, and training to be able to learn to know His voice.

In John 10, Jesus shares a parable about the good shepherd. He is careful to tell us that the sheep know the voice of their shepherd. Then He explains that He is the good shepherd and we are His sheep, and He again reiterates that His sheep "know him" and "listen to his voice."

The best way to begin to know God's voice is to immerse yourself in the Bible. Through God's Word you will gradually come to know the way God thinks and feels. His character and attitudes are all revealed in His Word to us. Everything God says to us will line up with His Word, but we must know Scripture in order to have a plumb line to measure our thoughts against. It is our guide in all matters.

D.L. Moody once said that the best way to show that a stick is crooked is not to argue about it or to spend time denouncing it, but to lay a straight stick alongside it. The best way we have of exposing the "rocks" we've been trying to pass off as God's voice is to lay them next to the Word of God. It will reveal their true value.

Prayer will never replace the Word of God as a source of knowledge about God. The two need to be used together. In addition, God uses teaching and sermons that are based on the Word, and often He will bring Scripture to your attention which will contain the answer you are seeking, the comfort you need, or the instruction you desire.

Interacting with God in relational prayer and growing in your knowledge of God through His Word will help you to begin to discern what is and what isn't the voice of God. It is not always an easy task and you will make mistakes. But as long as you are open to correction and willing to learn, you will soon be able to throw away the "rocks," keeping only those words of true value.

In watching people learn in this area, it is easy to spot the ones who are so certain they know God's voice and certain God is telling them this and that. They think every thought that enters their mind is from God.

It just doesn't work that way. God leads us by His Spirit within us, and most of our direction comes without a lot of conscious thought. More than specific words or sentences running across the screen of our mind, the Spirit's direction seems to come from somewhere deep within, gradually forming into impressions.

God may speak words into our mind from time to time, and in quiet moments of reflection we may hear His voice. He may even interrupt our thoughts to speak to us, but this is the exception rather than the rule. Normally God directs and speaks to us through His Word and through inner impressions from the Holy Spirit.

Years ago I began to test the things that I thought were from God. I started checking them out against the Word. I wrote them down and then kept track. Soon I began to see how vulnerable I was to error. It brought me back to God in anguished prayer for help. I began to pray earnestly that I would learn to know His voice, and I stopped assuming that I already did.

One of the most valuable lessons we can learn is that both our own carnal mind and Satan know how to mimic God's voice. We are susceptible to deception because of our own desires and needs, and until we learn to measure all those thoughts we think are from God against Scripture, we are very vulnerable.

I recently listened to a veteran missionary sharing some experiences in prayer. She had been a missionary for more than 40 years and was extremely knowledgeable about God and His ways. But what struck me most was her unwillingness to accept impressions or things that God told her without question.

Several stories she related involved God directing her to do something that was new for her. In each instance she described, she continued to spend more time in prayer, more time waiting to be sure. At times she even called someone else to pray before she stepped out and acted on what she felt God was saying.

This wise saint knew what so many Christians have failed to learn—her own vulnerability to error. It is true that these were important matters, so she was more careful than she would have been if she had just received some gentle words of encouragement, but her example is one we should all follow.

Learning to know God's voice is a vital part of our relational prayer life. It should be one of the most acute desires of our heart. But until we have confronted the inclination of our own fleshly nature to speak thoughts into our mind, we will continue to make grave mistakes and we will not learn to truly know God's voice. This is why it is important to deal with God—talking to Him, questioning, asking for help and going back over the things we thought He said to see if they really were from Him.

God's voice to us is precious. We must never demean it or cheapen it. He wants us to learn the difference between thoughts that are from Him and those that are throw-away "rocks." He wants to share Himself with us. God is careful to guard us as we stumble about learning to know Him—and we will come to know God's voice so that we don't have to continually worry and question.

> And the words of the Lord are flawless, like silver refined in a furnace of clay.
> —Psalm 12:6

Reflect

> *The voice of the Spirit of God is as gentle as a summer breeze—so gentle that unless you are living in complete fellowship and oneness with God, you will never hear it. The sense of warning and restraint that the spirit gives comes to us in the most amazing gentle ways. And if you are not sensitive enough to detect His voice, you will quench it, and your spiritual life will be impaired.*
> —Oswald Chambers

Have you learned to distinguish God's voice from the "noise" of your own emotions, desires, and thoughts?

Do you want to hear and know God's voice?

This isn't as obvious as it seems. Remember the reaction of the children of Israel at Mt. Sinai when God spoke to them. They were frightened and uncomfortable and told Moses to go listen for them. Part of learning to know God is *wanting* to hear Him speak to us, and learning to distinguish His voice from our own thoughts: the voice of our own emotions, desires, and will.

Study

What does Isaiah 42:2 and I Kings 19:11-13 tell us about the voice of God?

_____

What does Psalm 46:10 say we need to do in order to know God?

_____

What does Proverbs 8:34 say are the actions of a man who listens to God?

_____

What promise in Jeremiah 33:3 does God give to those who want to hear from Him?

_____

Receiving God's Voice

It takes time to learn to discern God's voice from our own thoughts, but God wants you to know His voice. There is a spiritual listening that can be cultivated. This is where open communication is so important—talking to God about the things you think He is saying, keeping track in a journal, and being honest when you've blown it.

This is a very subjective learning experience, but it can be exciting and wonderful.

If you are struggling with knowing God's voice, ask God to help you use His Word more. Select portions of scripture to read more slowly, contemplating the words, learning to read with your heart as well as your mind.

> *"Select a portion of Scripture—a verse, a paragraph, a chapter—and read it over and over. Think of Him as present and speaking to you, disclosing His mind and emotions and will. God is articulate:*

What Does God Sound Like?

He speaks to us through His Word. Meditate on His words until His thoughts begin to take shape in your mind.

When we read His Word we are reading His mind—what He knows; what He feels; what He wants; what He enjoys; what He desires; what He loves; what He hates.

Take time to reflect on what He is saying. Think about each word. Give yourself time for prayerful contemplation until God's heart is revealed and your heart is exposed."
—David Roper (*Psalm 23—The Song of a Passionate Heart*)

From now on, expect God to speak to you from His Word. He will use whatever text you are reading. Just be open to seeing personal encouragement, guidance, promises, and instruction in the text you are reading. The Holy Spirit can make Scripture relevant to you and speak to you even in an obscure text that normally wouldn't seem to relate to you at all.

Begin to underline the scriptures that speak to you personally and write them in your journal. God will speak to you through His Word!

Look up and underline Psalm 119:25-38. Make this passage your prayer this week.

Discussion

Do you have a story about a time you knew God was speaking to your heart, either through an inner impression or a scripture?

What did you learn through that experience?

God speaks to those who are in an attitude of listening; whose hearts are stilled and centered upon Him.
—Oswald Chambers

CHAPTER 14

When We Wander

"Watch that little girl over there."

Chuck nudged me and pointed toward the little blonde-haired girl with long pigtails walking down the center aisle of the department store. Eyes dreamy and unfocused, she was just walking, not noticing where she was or where she was going. Fortunately, her mother was only a few feet ahead and would patiently keep turning to check on her.

"Doesn't she remind you of Jula when she was that age?" Chuck asked.

The little girl was probably four or five years old. I looked at her a little more closely and then shrugged. "Not really." Except for the blonde pigtails, there wasn't a lot of similarity.

"Just watch her," Chuck urged again. "Jula used to do the same thing."

I looked over again and realized Chuck was referring to her actions more than her looks.

"Don't you remember?" he continued. "She would walk through a store completely unaware of us or where she was going. She would never, ever think to keep us in her vision, and soon she would just wander off."

I smiled at him as we both pictured Jula at that age, so cute and yet so exasperating. I remembered all too well the times I had lost her and frantically had to search through stores. I finally realized that no matter how much I cautioned, I would have to be responsible for keeping her beside me. She just couldn't seem to remember; her mind was too full of other things. And so I became constantly vigilant, always keeping my eye on her, making sure she stayed by my side.

Chuck, however, felt he could train her to be different. Since shopping was something he didn't particularly care for, he put all his energy into working with Jula. Whenever he was in a store with her, he would let her walk off. Then, keeping out of sight, he'd follow her until suddenly she would look around and notice we were gone.

As soon as he saw her start to panic, he would step into view and proceed to lecture her. "See, Jula, you weren't paying any attention. You just walked right off again. You can't do that!"

Sometimes in his zeal to teach her he would let her wait a while before revealing that he was there. Soon they'd come back to where I was, Jula tearful and chastened and Chuck comforting and scolding her at the same time, wiping away her tears with his big handkerchief and telling me how far she had wandered before she became aware that she wasn't with us.

Jula is grown up now, and we don't lose her in stores anymore, but Chuck's seeing the little girl in pigtails brought that era of our lives vividly back to our minds.

I thought about how like our relationship with God it was. We too tend to walk off from God—not deliberately, not in premeditated intent, but in simple carelessness because we just can't stay focused on Him.

We are sometimes too spiritually immature to realize how much is at risk, too inexperienced to understand the eternal dynamics of our careless actions, and too unacquainted with God to value a close walk with Him. We let our attention become caught by other things: our career, our hobbies, our family, or even our ministry. We become caught up in the world at hand and we wander off.

But our heavenly Father, just like our earthly parents, is vigilant. He keeps His eye on us and continues to reach out and pull us to Himself again and again. Sometimes, when we start to mature and need to accept our part in the relationship, He does as Chuck did. He follows along after us, keeping His eye on us, waiting for us to realize we've wandered off. Then, depending on how much we can be taught at that time, He may allow us to flounder a bit, calling out, searching, looking, before He steps back into view and picks us up, wiping our tears with His big handkerchief and comforting us. He reminds us that

He was there all along, and then begins to teach us how to do better next time.

God wants us to learn to stay by His side. We wander off because we are still so caught up in our own pursuits—our own thoughts. We are unaware of the dynamics of the relationship we can have with God, unaware of the possibilities, unaware of the magnitude of its effect on us, and unaware of God Himself.

Our heavenly Father wants us to mature into a full relationship with Him. He is eager to reveal Himself. He is eager to enjoy the pleasures that come from spending time with those He created simply for fellowship.

And so He draws us. He calls us to prayer. He uses our circumstances, our hopes and dreams, our problems, and our needs to cause us to come to Him. When we come, while we are focused on Him, He can reveal Himself to us. He can begin, little by little, to build within us the knowledge of what He is like and what He wants to do for us. We begin to recognize the pleasure of His companionship, and we want to experience it more often. When that happens, His desire for relationship with us can be fulfilled, and He can begin to teach us how to follow closely.

When we begin to grow in our relationship with God through intimate, consistent times of prayer, we will learn to deal with God in a relational way. This makes possible the kind of interaction necessary for intimacy and at the same time, begins to bring about change in us.

Our walk with God becomes more important—not because it is a habit, not because we believe in God and the Bible, and not because we think of God as a kind of crutch, available when we need Him. Our relationship with God becomes the very center of our existence, drawing us to live with Him, to work with Him, and to serve Him, because nothing else could possibly bring the joy and fulfillment that God Himself brings.

God desires to be known by man. He is fully aware of His own greatness, of His own indescribable wonder. And He wants to share Himself with us, knowing that as we come to truly know Him, we cannot help but love and adore Him; we cannot help but be drawn to receive the love and compassion He can pour out upon us.

Learning to Pray

There was an article in a Christian magazine a few years ago titled "Why Ministers Fall." The author stated that he had never seen one minister guilty of moral failure who kept a daily, personal devotion time in his walk with the Lord.

In the next issue, I was glancing through the letters to the editor and noticed one from a reader who disagreed with that statement. He felt that it was too simplistic, that a prayer-a-day-keeps-the-devil-away approach was a trite solution to a complex problem. He felt there were more dynamics involved than just prayer.

It made me think. Was prayer too easy an answer? If a prayer relationship with God will not keep us from falling, what will?

Prayer is the key, but it is the kind of prayer that makes the difference. Perhaps prayer-a-day devotions wouldn't be enough to keep a person from falling into sin, and the kind of praying that is simply a recital of our needs and the needs of the people and world around us, no matter how noble the prayers, won't be enough either. But I am convinced that relational prayer will. Relational prayer is the answer to our tendency to wander off, our tendency to allow the stresses of life to pull us away, and our inclination to get caught up in situations out of our control.

Perhaps the letter writer did not really think of prayer in this way. Many people do not.

If prayer is designed to draw people into a personal and intimate relationship with God, to teach man to know God personally, face to face, then in that intimate knowing of God there should be an intimate knowing of ourselves, an opening of ourselves to God in such a way that He is free to develop in us the kind of relationship with Him that will keep us from wandering off and lift us out of the cycles of defeat in which many Christians are caught. It should expose our sinfulness and our capacity for sin. It should head off the problem areas and guard our footsteps. It should open up the inner rooms of our heart to the cleansing, healing light of Christ, so that we can be changed and protected from falling.

When We Wander

God's Word makes some powerful promises about His keeping power:

> Being confident of this, that *he who began a good work in you will carry it on to completion* until the day of Christ Jesus.
> —Philippians 1:6, emphasis added

> To him who is able to keep you from falling and to present you before his glorious presence without fault and with great joy—to the only God our Savior be glory, majesty, power and authority, through Jesus Christ our Lord, before all ages, now and forever-more! Amen.
> —Jude 1:24-25

Relational prayer opens us to the interaction that is necessary if we are to grow and change. Direct confrontation with God leaves no room for accidently wandering off. In this kind of relationship we will find all the direction we need for our personal growth. God will always be faithful to deal with the areas that trip us up. He will always guide us onto the right path, and He will always provide grace to enable us to do what He requires of us.

When we come repeatedly to Christ with our needs, He begins a threefold work in us.

First, He draws us close so that when we seek His help, He can begin to reveal Himself as an intimate friend and a burden bearer. We find solace and help in Him, and at the same time we begin to experience deep contentment. We will learn to know God through our time spent with Him.

Second, He uses the times we are driven to Him by our circumstances to work in us: to reveal the parts of our nature that continue to cause upheavals, whether it is sin, our own driving ambitions and motives, our insecurities or emotional scars, or simply our spiritual immaturity.

Third, He begins to teach us His principles and show us His ways in greater measure, so we can experience His life in ever-deeper ways.

Because prayer is designed to further our relationship, we can feel free to question Him when help does not come. It means that instead of the answer we hoped for, we may receive teaching or correction, or simply grace to keep going during difficulties.

In relational prayer we begin to try out the promises of God's Word to see if they are true—coming to God over and over and asking until we understand His ways.

In relational prayer we begin to find out what is God's voice and what is not; we begin to exchange our understanding for His, gradually giving up our distorted thinking and taking on His truth.

In relational prayer we give God the opportunity to deal with us, exposing the sin nature that keeps getting in the way of the relationship, clearing up old misconceptions of Him that have weighed us down for so many years, and healing us of past hurts.

In relational prayer God reveals His great love to us again and again, building in us confidence in Him, and contentment and joy that surpasses anything we could ever have imagined.

Reflect

Are you easily distracted from God's side?

Have you been a seeker of God in the past and then failed to keep up the same level of intensity? What drew you away?

Perhaps your Christian lifestyle keeps your wandering from being obvious to others but "your own way" has involved keeping God at a safe distance, refusing to deal with Him in prayer, or keeping the relationship on a surface level.

Can you see how this can also be wandering?

Study

The Bible uses the analogy of sheep when describing children of God.

In Isaiah 53:6 what do we do that is like sheep? _____

What does the second line say? _____

When We Wander

What does that phrase mean to you personally? _____

In 1 Peter 2:25, Peter uses the same phrase in his letter to Christians.

Have you been guilty of moving or going "your own way?" _____

What kinds of distractions cause you to wander? _____

_____

In Mark 4:18-19, what did Jesus say happens to some people?

_____

_____

Point to Ponder

Many of the problems we live in—depression, relationship difficulties, unconquered sins—would be resolved if we learned to deal with God, opening ourselves up by coming to Him in honesty: honesty about what we think and feel, honesty about our circumstances, honesty about other people, and honesty about God Himself.

Receiving God's Call to Relationship

God wants you to know Him. He wants to share Himself with you, and He wants you to become so wrapped up in Him that knowing Him defines your very existence.

Look up and meditate on the following scriptures:

Song of Solomon 2:14

Jeremiah 30:21b

Jeremiah 33:3

Think of these scriptures as a personal invitation from God.

What is your response?

Will you make a new commitment today? To become a seeker of God, one who deals with Him on a real and intimate level?

> Dear Father God,
>
> I have been prone to wander from Your side. Forgive me. I am so easily distracted by my own interests and pursuits, and I know I have been guilty of allowing even the good things in my life to draw me away from You. Forgive me for that and help me. Please continue to draw me into a closer relationship.
>
> And Lord, I want to begin to deal with You in an honest way. I want to open myself up to You and be willing to talk to You about everything. Take my life. I commit myself to You and to a more open and honest relationship with You.
> Amen.

Discussion

Discuss what you have learned or found enlightening from this section of the book. Was thinking of prayer as a way to build your relationship with God a new thought for you?

Walking with God

I am gentle and humble in heart,
and you will find rest for your souls,
—Matthew 11:29

CHAPTER 15

What God Really Wants

Jeb and his wife, Martha, settled down on their new land, built a cabin, a barn, and a corral for their live stock. Then Zeb hung a big bell in a tree and explained, "There are renegades around here, Martha. If you need me, ring the bell—but only in an emergency."

Days later, as Zeb was riding out to the fields to cut wood, he heard the bell ring. He headed home at full gallop.

"What's wrong?"

"I just thought maybe you'd like some fresh coffee," Martha said.

"Tarnation, woman, I said the bell was for emergencies. Half the day's gone, and I still have chores to do."

Once more he rode out. Just as he picked up the ax, he heard the bell. Again he raced home.

"The washtub's leaking," reported Martha.

"That ain't no blasted emergency! I've gotta cut the wood."

Two hours later Zeb was chopping down a tree when the bell rang again. He charged home to find the cabin in flames, the barn burned to the ground, and his cattle stampeding away. Then he found Martha, slumped near the bell, with an arrow in her shoulder.

"Now, Martha," Zeb exclaimed, "this is more like it!"

Some of us have a sneaking suspicion that God is a little bit like Zeb. We may never formulate the specific thought that God is interested only in major concerns, but a part of us may still feel that He has a lot of work to do—He's got a big world full of big problems, and He gave us the "bell" of prayer for those times when we really need help.

We had better not ring it unless we've got something important to say. Prayer is only for important matters, intercessory concerns, and perhaps some praise and thanksgiving.

It isn't just people who are ignorant of God's Word who feel this way. There are people with doctorates in theology who have studied the Bible for years and engaged in countless debates about God and His ways, and still missed the simplicity of God's purpose and design for mankind.

Some people get so caught up in the vastness of God's world or the hugeness of the world's problems, or so enamored with profound debates and intellectual grappling with biblical truths that they fail to grasp the dailiness, the intimacy, the personal nature of a true relationship with God.

Throughout this book we have seen that prayer was designed by God as a way to establish a relationship with you and me. To discover the right attitude about God and our communication with Him, we must go back to the essential reason for our very existence.

One of the great creeds of the church, the Westminster Shorter Catechism, states that "the chief end of man is to know God and enjoy Him forever." That God created mankind for fellowship is affirmed throughout Scripture:

> You have made known to me the path of life; you will fill me with joy in your presence, with eternal pleasures at your right hand.
> —Psalm 16:11

> And now, Israel, what does the Lord your God require of you, but to fear the Lord your God, to walk in all His ways, and to love Him, and to serve the Lord your God with all your heart and with all your soul.
> —Deuteronomy 10:12 NKJV

God desires to relate to us in a way that extends throughout every area of our life. How different this is from our natural tendency to put everything in our life into two different compartments: spiritual and nonspiritual, or "important to God" and "unimportant."

What God Really Wants

We Christians often try to live in two worlds, a spiritual one a few minutes a day (perhaps a little longer on Sundays) and a physical one the rest of the time. We don't feel we can be a part of both simultaneously. We aren't sure how to bring one into the other, or whether we should even try, so we try to keep them distinct. We pigeonhole aspects of our lives into separate slots: spiritual or physical, religious or secular, eternal or temporal.

We know that God wants to develop the fruit of the Spirit in us and help us be a reflection of Christ to our world, but we may still fail to see any spiritual relevance to our physical world, or a way to bring the two worlds together.

We take on "spiritual" pursuits like witnessing or teaching a Sunday School class in an endeavor to fulfill the commands of Christ and the New Testament. These are the things we do to obey God and please Him. We think of these activities as somewhat "holy."

The ordinary, day-by-day part of life—our job, mopping the floor, watching a football game, giving the dog a bath—is necessary, but it has no "eternal" meaning or value, and we feel God isn't really interested in it.

Consequently a close walk with God is something we save for later—after we take care of all the other necessary, but nonspiritual, things in our lives. We may look forward to the time when our relationship with God will have more depth, more involvement, but unless we are in full-time ministry, we don't really see that kind of life as a viable option for us. So we plug along, living our life in a kind of balancing act with job, family, and personal interests on one side and our love for God and our Christian activities on the other. The two sides don't meet very often, but we may feel that God is busy with other things anyway, or that He is waiting for us to finish with the physical, necessary activities before He spends time with us.

But that is like saying a loving father or mother isn't interested in any part of his or her child's life except the chores the child does. Think of the very best, most involved parent you know. Then think about God. He is our heavenly Father and is a perfect parent to us in every way.

The truth is that God wants to enjoy you and be with you, not just when you're praying for a half hour in the morning or reading a Bible story to your son, and not just when you are in full-time ministry or involved in spiritual pursuits—God wants to be with you, to enjoy your companionship now.

You will never understand this until you learn what is important to God—that He values you, not what you do.

He desires to walk close to you continually, to participate in all of your life. He is not interested just in the "spiritual" side. To Him, it is all spiritual because you were created a spiritual being. When you accepted Christ you were indwelt by His Spirit. You were divinely created and placed in a divinely created world, and everything about you and your life is, in one sense, sacred.

Man's relationship with God was disrupted by sin, but physical life still contains the hallowed stamp of God. God's plan of redemption through Jesus Christ gives it further value, further vibrancy, as He enables us through His grace to live in Him in the world He created.

Until we begin to understand God's true attitude toward us and our implicit value to Him because of who we are, our thinking will be distorted. Consequently, we will be unable to enjoy God's presence and help in all of our life.

Our walk with God is to be experienced today, just the way we are, in just the circumstances we are in right now. This means learning to walk with God through all of the ordinary moments as well as the moments we've considered spiritual in the past. It means learning that God is part of

> walking the dog
> > driving to work
> > > bathing the baby
> > > > and waiting through the endless lines at the Department of Motor Vehicles

as well as the moments of

singing worship choruses
    witnessing to a neighbor
        praying for souls in Africa
            and teaching a Sunday School class
                to a bunch of rowdy eight-year-old boys.

Unlike Zeb, God isn't upset when we "ring the bell" because we want to talk to Him about any part of our ordinary life. God wants us to learn to know Him intimately. In order for this kind of relationship to develop, we must become aware of God's interest, His concern, and His willingness to participate in the whole of our lives.

This happens as we begin to see prayer as a means of communication with God and an opportunity to know Him. As we participate in a vital prayer relationship, we will gradually become aware of God's concern and interest in more than just the aspects of our lives we think of as "spiritual." When we begin to recognize the need and the privilege of being with Him in all the activities of our day, our morning devotions will become much more than time "set aside for God"; they will become just the beginning of our communion with God for the whole day.

Andrew Murray explains it well in an excerpt from his book, *The Believer's Daily Renewal*:

> What a difference it would make in the life of many if everything in the closet [devotional time] were subordinate to this one thing: I want throughout the day to walk with God; my morning hour is the time when my Father enters into a definite agreement with me and I with Him that it shall be so. What strength would be imparted by the consciousness that God has taken charge of me, He Himself is going with me; I am going to do His will all day in His strength; I am ready for all that may come. What nobility would come into life if secret prayer were not only an asking for some new sense of comfort, or light or strength, but also the surrendering of life just for one day into the sure and safe keeping of a mighty and faithful God.

God is ready to show you a new side of His nature if you have not yet experienced it: His interest and concern in all of your life and His desire to share it all with you.

> As you have therefore received Christ Jesus the Lord, so walk in Him.
> —Colossians 2:6 NKJV

Reflect

The chief end of man is to know God and to enjoy Him forever.
—Westminster Shorter Catechism

Have you learned to enjoy God?

Do you make Him a part of your everyday life?

Do you feel He cares about it?

Study

Deuteronomy 12:18b instructs us to rejoice before the Lord in _____

According to Colossians 3:17, what should we do in the name of Jesus?
_____

In what does Proverbs 3:6 tell us to acknowledge God? _____

What are some practical, non-spiritual events Jesus was involved in during His time on earth?

Luke 5:1-7 _____

John 2:1-12 _____

Matthew 17:24-27 _____

Mark 6:30-39 _____

Read Matthew 11:29. In light of the above scriptures, what do you think the word "humble" or "lowly" means?_____

What do Psalms 74:16 and 118:24 say about our "days?"_____
_____

Meditate on the above verses. Think about the fact that your day belongs to God.

Receiving God in Our Days

> Then God promises to love me all day,
> sing songs all through the night!
> My life is God's prayer.
> —Psalm 42:8 (THE MESSAGE)

We need to remember that as spiritual beings, there is a continuous eternal or divine touch upon all of our ordinary endeavors.

Think about this truth and try to grasp what it means to you. During the week, while you are doing routine things, endeavor to see it in a spiritual context. Bring God into it.

Increase your quiet time this week and include talking to God about your daily, practical activities.

Ask God to enlarge your understanding to be able to grasp His presence in the ordinary moments of your life.

Prayer of Response

Dear Heavenly Father,

I know, as my Father, You care about my ordinary life. Please help me to begin walking with You throughout my day. Teach me how to share my whole life with You. I want to know Your presence in all my life. Thank You for Your faithfulness in teaching me Your ways.

Amen.

Discussion

Share some of the ways you brought God into your everyday life this week.

> Come to me. Get away with me and you'll recover your life. I'll show you how to take a real rest. Walk with me and work with me—watch how I do it. Learn the unforced rhythms of grace.
> I won't lay anything heavy or ill-fitting on you. Keep company with me and you'll learn to live freely and lightly.
> —Matthew 11:28-29 (THE MESSAGE)

CHAPTER 16

The Beauty of the Ordinary

It was fall and I was sitting on the sidelines of a soccer field watching my son (just as I had every fall for the last 11 years). It was the first game of the season, and I was thinking about how many of these games I had attended throughout the years.

I watched Matt as he executed a perfect pass, wondering again if his goal of playing soccer for a college team was attainable. He was 17 and we were caught up in the flurry of college applications, SAT tests, career choices, and future plans.

As I sat watching him play, I whispered a little prayer. "God, give us wisdom. You know what is best for his life."

Then I thought, "Maybe all this emphasis on soccer is a waste of time."

Turning my heart toward God again, I silently asked, "What do You think about it, Father?"

I remembered my prayer time that morning. I had been so burdened to pray for people in Indonesia who had yet to be reached with the gospel. I had also prayed about a crisis in Liberia that was claiming hundreds of lives, many of whom had probably never heard about Jesus.

As I thought about the seriousness of those situations and the magnitude of the needs in the world for spiritual help, I wondered about the value of even watching a soccer game as I was doing now. I wondered about my son, his activities and plans, and what he would do with his life.

Could anything be as important as the kinds of things I had prayed about that morning? Wasn't all this soccer activity pretty irrelevant and perhaps even out of place?

Of course, soccer was just the outlet for my real question, which probed further into the division we make between the "spiritual" and "non-spiritual" areas of our lives: "Is there any value in any activity that doesn't speak to the overwhelming spiritual needs of the world around us?"

And I wondered for the hundredth time, "God, what is Your perspective on this? How do we find spiritual balance in our lives? How do we justify anything in our life that takes time away from meeting the massive spiritual needs of the world? Shouldn't that consume our thoughts, our lives?"

How could I write a chapter on God being interested and concerned in the ordinary events, even my son's interest in soccer? It seemed so frivolous and without purpose in the light of the kind of things I had prayed about that morning.

As I asked God to give me understanding and to show me His ways, I thought again about the principles of relationship He had been teaching me for the past 15 years of my life. My mind automatically went back to the reason for our existence: "to know God and enjoy Him forever."

When God formed the earth and created mankind to live in it, the purpose was to give God the opportunity to be involved with another being, someone who would come into the relationship of his or her own volition and willingly participate in an intimate, mutually loving, and interactive alliance. God's reason for creating us was not to use us to save a lost world.

We were to live and work, connected to God by His Spirit and able to enjoy Him and the abundant life He desired to give us. We were to use the various abilities and talents given us to create and enjoy a harmonious and pleasurable life on earth. It would be made complete by our connection and interaction with God. The beauty of our lives would be a reflection of Him, His glory, His power, and His greatness.

Yet sin brought an abrupt end to that kind of existence and ushered in a completely different reality, making it necessary for our lives to take on another purpose as well—that of reclaiming through Christ what was lost because of sin. Sin caused the path to an intimate relationship with God to become much more complex.

The work of reclamation, however, does not negate God's original purpose for our existence. Even though Christian service (intercession, witnessing, helping, etc.) should be a part of every life truly committed to Christ, we are still to glory in our ordinary life lived in Him.

If we forget God's participation in the ordinary moments, we will miss the point entirely. We will fail to grasp the purpose behind the creation of man, the death and resurrection of Christ, the indwelling and empowerment of man by the Spirit of God, and the very reason God tells us to go into all the world and preach the gospel—to give God the opportunity to be connected again with mankind.

When we offer ourselves as a living sacrifice to God and choose to live in submission to His Spirit within us, we will find that He does not intend to take over our faculties and make us into little robots to use to carry out His goals in the world.

Our ordinary lives, our unique abilities, and our individual interests and pursuits bring color, variation, and pleasure to God. He doesn't want to submerge us. He simply wants to walk with us. He wants to enlarge our capabilities, He wants to help us, and above all, He wants to restore the relationship with man that was lost because of sin.

There will be times of spiritual emphasis when our whole being—spirit, soul and body—is caught up in the pursuit of God or in response to Him during times of worship, intercession, or ministry. But these are not the only times we please Him or gain His attention. His eye is upon us every moment and the "spiritual" aspect of our lives is simply the time He ordained to acquaint us with Himself, which is necessary if we are ever to become the complete beings He created us to be, and necessary if we are to ever allow Him full access to our lives.

The "spiritual" aspects of our lives will indeed grow as our individual spirits are energized by being joined to His Spirit. This growth will then be reflected in other aspects of day-to-day living, realigning those areas with the order and wisdom of God's original plan.

Our dealings with God will begin to expose our carnal nature, the real motives behind many of our actions, the distortions, and the wrong emphasis we place on so many things. But as God brings our lives back into proper alignment and focus, He will not rob us of our fun, our individuality, and our enjoyment of life. Actually, He wants to help us throw off the carnality and sin that steal joy from us.

When we begin to allow Him into our days to walk beside us, we'll find His presence isn't there to quench the fun or stop our ordinary activities, but to bring joy, to bring deliverance from the problems we create when left to ourselves, to give help and direction, to provide new and better ways of doing things. He wants to add a touch of the divine to your life and to mine. He wants to enlarge our lives with His presence.

Without this foundational understanding, we become out of balance, prone to distorted thinking, and unable to fulfill God's foremost purpose for us: to walk with Him now, in the world He created for us, and throughout eternity. We tend to get mired in the day-to-day aspects of life and fail to see its eternal significance, or we become so "spiritual" or caught up in spiritual pursuits that we lose touch with the reality of God in the "everydays."

We look at life as if it were two separate puzzles that God handed us and told us to make into one picture.

What kind of parents would mix up two puzzles and then hand the pieces to a small child, telling him to put them together into one picture while they stood quietly by to watch the confusion, the frustration, and the discouragement?

Yet many people feel God has handed us that kind of puzzle. We are busy struggling with a physical life and a spiritual life that just don't seem to fit together. But our problem isn't that we've got two different and separate puzzles. Our problem is that we think we do.

Underneath all our striving to operate in the day-to-day world and still keep God happy is the pervasive belief that this is just the way it is and will always be until we get to heaven—God is only really concerned in the eternal and spiritual aspects of our lives and we, out of necessity (and desire) are interested in the earthly.

We feel that on earth we simply have to put up with the ordinary aspects while trying to please God in the spiritual activities. It's made more difficult because we are drawn so naturally to the earthly part. Ball games, parties, and shopping often seem like more fun than the activities we think God cares about: Bible reading, prayer, and witnessing.

So we struggle with our puzzle pieces, never coming to the realization that God doesn't view our physical and spiritual life as two separate puzzles. He didn't create life that way at all.

In reality, He created one beautiful picture with both aspects of our lives-physical and spiritual-fitting perfectly together, each enhancing the other and each giving the other an added dimension. He doesn't care more about Bible reading than our "fun" activities. It just seems that way because it's often the only time we make Him part of our lives.

We see our daily routine—getting ready for work, grappling with problems at the job, washing clothes, and mowing the lawn—as boring and mundane, but necessary. We see our pleasurable activities as God-given perhaps, but still separate. We look at our Christian service as the only really valuable thing (at least to God) that we do, and our Bible reading and prayer time as requirements expected of us by God. We end up viewing life with God as an exercise in shuffling puzzle parts.

Each of us needs a new perspective. We need to be pulled up next to God so we can see life from a different point of view. When we begin to walk with God throughout the whole of our life, we will be able to receive His sight, His way of seeing the puzzle of life He has handed to us, and we'll learn that everything fits together beautifully.

God wants us to fully comprehend and use the beauty and value of both worlds, spiritual and physical, just as He does. Without God we are unable to fully grasp either one. We become mired in our "self" with all the limits, problems, constrictions, and narrowness of view that "self" imposes.

Walking with God and receiving His perspective accomplishes two things: it reminds us of what is truly important and, at the same time, infuses the daily routine with a touch of the extra ordinary, the divine.

> And whatever you do, whether in word or deed, do it all in the name of the Lord Jesus, giving thanks to God the Father through him.
> —Colossians 3:17

Reflect

One of the most amazing revelations of God comes to us when we learn that it is in the everyday things of life that we realize the magnificent deity of Jesus Christ.
　　　—Oswald Chambers *(My Utmost for His Highest)*

Do you think about God being part of the mundane areas of your life?

Do you feel He is interested?

Study

Read John 21:1-14

Think about what Jesus does in this story.

What is the first thing Jesus asks his disciples?_____

What practical thing did He do for them that morning? (verse 9)

_____

Meditate on this section of scripture, thinking about Christ's physical actions. Use your imagination to picture Him with the disciples: calling to them in the boat, cooking for them, serving them breakfast...

What does Zechariah 4:10 tell us not to do?

What are some of the small things your Heavenly Father is interested in?

Deuteronomy 29:5_____

2 Kings 6:1-7_____

Matthew 10:29_____

Luke 12:28_____

The Beauty of the Ordinary

In Matthew 10:42, what "small thing" did Jesus say He would take note of? _____

Receiving Small Things from God

This week,

1) Talk to God about some of the practical aspects of your life.

2) Thank Him for a small, mundane item or happening.

3) Ask for help with something practical.

Use your journal to record some of those moments.

Discussion

Relate to your group any new attempts to pray about small matters.

> *We look for visions from heaven and for earthshaking events to see God's power... Yet we never realize that all the time God is at work in our everyday events and in the people around us.*
> —Oswald Chambers (*My Utmost for His Highest*)

CHAPTER 17

Should I Pray About It?

Understanding God's interest in our everyday lives still leaves us with some practical questions. What kinds of things should I pray about? At what point on the scale—from asking for a new pair of shoes to praying for the missionaries in Africa—does the Lord start listening?

Should I ask God for a parking space during the Christmas rush at the mall? Should I pray for help in getting through my overcrowded schedule? Should I ask God for that new dress?

Does He care? Will He answer?

These kinds of questions about prayer that involve our everyday lives lead us to questions about God Himself.

Second Kings 6 relates a fascinating tale about Elisha and some of his fellow prophets. They were chopping down trees to build some dwellings. As one of them was hacking away, the iron ax head flew off the handle of his ax and dropped into some water.

"Oh, no!" one of the young men cried. "It was borrowed."

Elisha immediately asked where it had fallen. The young man pointed to the area and then watched as Elisha walked over to a tree, cut a stick, and threw it into the water. The iron ax head, contrary to all laws of gravity, floated to the surface where he was able to retrieve it.

Undoubtedly the young prophet was astonished, but this was not really a big thing to God. To us the suspension of natural law is amazing—especially when you consider the reason: to recover an ax head.

In relation to all the "important" happenings of those days, losing an iron ax head was not something to be all that concerned about. Yet God was very willing to intervene and take care of the matter.

God cares about our daily lives. Jesus reminded us of this when He said, "Are not two sparrows sold for a penny? Yet not one of them will fall to the ground apart from the will of your Father. And even the very hairs of your head are all numbered. So don't be afraid; you are worth more than many sparrows" (Matthew 10:29-31).

He cautioned us not to worry about everyday matters such as food and clothing because if God "clothes the grass of the field, which is here today and tomorrow is thrown into the fire, will he not much more clothe you...?" (Matthew 6:30).

We might interpret this Scripture to mean we don't need to ask about these kinds of things. However, Paul tells us "in everything make your requests known to the Lord."

I would never spend time agonizing in prayer over a routine sales meeting, a parking space, or my desire for a new pair of shoes. It isn't that important. But I will talk to God about it. I do mention my everyday needs and desires to Him, because I believe if they concern me, they concern Him. It is in telling God about everything that concerns us that we can cease to worry over the matters.

When Jesus left the world, He promised to send the Holy Spirit to be our personal counselor and guide.

> I will ask the Father, and he will give you another Counselor to be with you forever—the Spirit of truth. The world cannot accept him, because it neither sees him nor knows him. But you know him, for he lives with you and will be in you.
>
> —John 14:16-17

The Holy Spirit of God resides in each of us. He literally walks with us, talks with us, sleeps with us, and is present with us at all times. It is His job to guide you and to be God's envoy to you.

We've already seen how the Holy Spirit helps us become more disciplined in our devotional life. As we begin to know Him and learn how easily He will share Himself with us and guide us into truth, we will learn to depend upon Him more and more in all the matters of our lives.

He is present within you. He knows what you are doing and thinking and, frankly, He might as well be involved in your "everydays."

The apostle Paul tells us to "walk in the Spirit" in response to our need to live the life of Christ day by day. Jesus promised that after He left He would send the Holy Spirit so that you and I could have His help and presence every day. The privilege of having the Holy Spirit indwell us is God's way of enabling us to walk with Him. God through His Spirit comes to literally live inside you and me, making possible the kind of day-by-day relationship He had in mind when He created us.

When God created man, He placed a spirit within to energize, direct, and motivate. God intended for man's spirit to be joined with His Spirit and in that union man's energizing and directing force would always reflect the nature of God. Man, however, was free to choose whether his own spirit would be joined with God—whether he would submit to God's Spirit or to his own strong capabilities. Adam's sin broke the union between God and man, and man chose to develop his own soul independent of God.

The soul (our mind, emotions, and will) has become so overdeveloped that even after accepting Christ and joining our spirit back to God, our soul still wants to continue to work independently. Because we have been "in control" for so long, we still want to use our own powerful abilities to manage our life.

It takes time to learn how to allow God's Spirit within us to become a part of all our lives. It takes time to understand how the Spirit of God can flow through us and be the energizing and covering force. However, when we begin to "give over" to the Spirit of God in our daily lives, we are submitting to the lordship of God. We are allowing Him to help us become what He designed us to be, and we are agreeing to do what He suggests.

God wants to walk with us throughout our life, day-by-day, moment-by-moment. Since He wants to be with us, He really doesn't mind helping us with our ordinary concerns. Most of our lives are made up of trying to make a living, dealing with others in interpersonal relationships, washing dishes, disciplining our children, and driving in commute traffic.

God's Spirit, residing in us, is a part of all of this, and He can make a difference. He's with you—while you struggle with that accounting error, in the crowded line at the supermarket, while you watch your son's Little League game, or as you tussle with the weeds in your backyard. Wouldn't it be silly not to involve Him?

As we become more aware of His presence with us, we will naturally begin to turn to Him for help. It will become the easiest thing in the world to simply pray, "Help me find this error in the books, Father."

God delights in this kind of relationship with His children, and as we cooperate with His Spirit within us, He is free to make our paths smooth before us and help us in every way.

Jesus told us that we are not to worry over the mundane matters of our lives. As we go through our day, we can rely on His Spirit within us for His help, His direction, and His intervention as we turn our concerns over to Him.

We will soon find that our prayer life and our intimacy with God will not be confined to that half hour in the morning—it will begin to permeate all of our life!

The little book *Practicing the Presence of God* by Brother Lawrence is a series of thoughts on *every* moment of our lives being an opportunity for communication with God, so that in everything it is possible for our thoughts to easily go back to Him. With words of praise, requests for help, intercession for someone who comes to mind, and simple thoughts of Him, we begin to experience the presence of God in all of our lives.

When Paul said to "pray without ceasing," he knew it wouldn't be possible to constantly be in fervent prayer, and yet our minds and hearts can learn to be in tune with God throughout the day so that no matter what the focus of our attention is at that moment, He is welcome there.

Gradually there comes an overriding awareness of God and a desire to never shut Him out. We become acquainted with God enough to understand His dailiness, His interest, and His enjoyment in the whole of our lives—His participation in the fun, the work, and the leisure, as well as in the times of formal prayer and Bible study. Then we, like Brother Lawrence, begin to include God in everything we do. A glorious new aspect of the "abundant life" that Christ promised opens up to us. The presence of the Holy Spirit and His constant help is not something you will want to deny. It is one of the privileges of being a child of God.

God is ready to listen to you and help you throughout your day. He really does want to be involved with you. His Spirit residing in you can make a profound difference in the quality of your days as you learn to turn to Him for companionship and help in all the moments of your life.

> If we live in the Spirit, let us also walk in the Spirit.
> —Galatians 5:25 NKJV

> Praise be to the Lord, to God our Savior, who daily bears our burdens.
> —Psalm 68:19

Reflect

Are you having difficulty thinking that God is concerned about the ordinary moments of your life?

Have you grasped the fact that the Holy Spirit of God is present within you each moment?

> For what great nation is there that has a god so near to it, as the Lord our God is to us, for whatever reason we may call upon Him?
> —Deuteronomy 4:7 (NKJV)

Study

What does 1 Corinthians 3:16 tell us about the Holy Spirit?

Learning to Pray

What instruction does Galatians 5:25 give?
_____

What are some of the things the Holy Spirit does for us?

John 14:26, John 16:13 _____

Acts 1:8 _____

Romans 5:5 _____

Romans 8:16 _____

Romans 8:26 _____

Romans 15:13 _____

1 Corinthians 2:9-12 _____

1 Corinthians 12:4 _____

Galatians 5:22-23 _____

Do you know and experience the presence of Christ through the ministry of the Holy Spirit within you? (John 16:14) _____

Do you have gifts operating in and through you? (1 Corinthians 12:7-11)
_____

Is the fruit of the Spirit being manifested in your life? (Galatians 5:22-23) _____

Is your passion and love for God growing? (Romans 5:5) _____

Are you being changed into His likeness? (2 Corinthians 3:18) _____

Receiving the Holy Spirit of God

Spend some time this week talking to the Holy Spirit, thanking Him for His help and inviting Him to be in control of your life.

Should I Pray About It?

The Holy Spirit comes to dwell in each of us when we accept Christ as Savior, but there is much more available to believers as they yield themselves completely to God and ask for His Holy Spirit to completely fill them.

The Bible speaks of the Holy Spirit

- *with* us—John 14:16
- *in* us—John 14:17; 1 Corinthians 6:19
- *upon* us—Acts 1:4; Joel 2:28-29; Acts 10:44

Today, ask God to fill you with His Holy Spirit. Ask Him to live and work in you as He desires.

Try "practicing the presence" of God like Brother Lawrence during the week. Consciously share your day and your activities with Him.

Discussion

Share your experiences with "practicing the presence" of Christ with the rest of the group.

Did the person of the Holy Spirit become more real to you through this study of His activities in us and for us?

CHAPTER 18

God's Call

When Matthew was around three years old, I tucked him into bed and sat down next to him. Reaching for our already-worn copy of Bible Stories for Little Ones, I put my arm around him and opened the book. When I saw the story for that evening was about Samuel being called by God in the middle of the night, I thought, "Good, Matt will like this one."

I quickly got into the drama of it, using my experience as a storyteller in Sunday School to re-create the wonder and intrigue of this special event. I told him about Samuel as a young boy working and sleeping in the temple and about the night he heard a voice softly calling him as he slept.

"Samuel..."

I related how he kept running to Eli, convinced that he was the one calling him, until finally the old priest realized what was happening and told Samuel when he heard his name again to answer the voice with, "Here I am, Lord. I'm listening."

When I finished the story I felt I should talk to Matt about his need to learn to know God's voice. I told him that as he grew, God would want to talk to him, just like Samuel, and that he needed to listen and respond.

After talking about it for a few minutes, I paused and quietly asked, "What would you do if one night you heard God's voice saying, 'Matthew? ....Matthew?'"

Matt glanced up at me and hesitated. I could tell he was giving it a lot of thought.

Finally he answered, "I guess I'd say, 'What are you doing in my bed, God?'"

It had been a little unrealistic to expect a spiritual response from a three-year-old. But don't we as adults often answer God with just about the same reaction? Often our reply to God's call in our life is, "What are You doing here?"

There are moments when we become aware of God's presence enough to hear Him calling us, just as Samuel did. It may be through a particularly moving church service when the pastor reminds us of God's call for commitment and further surrender of our lives. It may be through a growing dissatisfaction with things the way they are. Or it may be through a storm of rough circumstances abruptly interrupting our smooth, self-centered sail through life.

Whatever way God uses to get your attention, at some point He will begin to call you, not just to a relationship and not just to a consistent prayer life, but to intimacy.

When He does, what will your response be?

God desires more than just a disciplined prayer life. He desires more than a knowledge of Him based on your extensive study of the Bible. He wants more than a commitment to soul-winning or Christian service. He wants to be so intimately close to you that you will begin to hear His very heartbeat.

For this to happen, however, you must respond to His call as He begins to speak your name throughout the moments of your life. Your response to His call will determine the path your relationship with God will take, whether you will be able to go on to deeper intimacy as Samuel did, or whether you will continue to live out your life holding God at arm's length and saying, "No closer."

We have already seen that our carnal nature will resist coming too close to God. This is true in the beginning of our relationship as we are trying to establish a prayer life, and it is also true when God begins to draw us to a closer walk.

Although we may see the purpose in "dealing with God" in prayer so that we learn to know Him, there still may be an imaginary line across our life that divides the areas in which we consult with God and those we take care of on our own. The usual reason we give is "God is interested in this, but not that," and we greet any kind of intrusion with the question, "What are You doing here, God?" Many things can cloud our view so that we are unable to see God as He is and to participate in a relationship in such a way that God is a part of *all* of our life.

Sometimes that imaginary line is drawn more for our convenience than concern that God is interested only in important matters. When we place God on a high and lofty plane and set up our personal rules for religion and worship, we can keep God at a distance; we can keep Him where we want Him. We can study about Him, discuss Him, debate theological differences, feel good about our religious pursuits, and still not relate to Him on a personal level. We can refuse to come to grips with the reality of His presence and refuse to allow the difference He wants to make in our lives in all that we are and all we do.

Although my philosophy about God and my worship may have all the outward trappings of piety, when I keep God in a distant and celestial place and shut Him off from huge areas of my life, my religion is really a shallow veneer covering a will still determined to retain control.

Keeping God behind that imaginary line means I am never faced with the need to submit to Him at all levels of my life. That is a powerful reason for a philosophy about God which says He is only concerned with exalted spiritual matters—salvation of souls in Africa and freedom for Christians in oppressed nations—but not my daily business decisions, my vacation plans, or my hobbies.

Because we are willing to walk with God most of the time, giving Him a part of our lives, even regularly spending time in prayer, we may be shocked when suddenly, in the midst of one of the areas in which we're walking on our own, we hear God's voice.

Just as God audibly called Samuel in the night, He also continues to call you to His side. He wants you to learn to walk beside Him. Next to Him, in that position of closeness, there will be opportunity for fellowship and for participation in each other's lives.

In Samuel's life we see a tremendous example of someone who walked with God. Several Scriptures point to the intimacy of their relationship.

First Samuel 3 describes Samuel's growing maturity in the Lord: "Samuel grew, and the Lord was with him, and *did let none of his words fall to the ground*" (v. 19 KJV, emphasis added).

A few chapters later it says, "Samuel heard all the words of the people, and he *rehearsed them in the ears of the Lord*" (8:21 KJV, emphasis added). Here we see a picture of Samuel sitting next to God, leaning over and whispering into His ear. The literal translation is "he talked them over with the Lord."

A further glimpse of the closeness God and Samuel shared is given in the next chapter: "*Now the Lord had told Samuel in his ear* a day before Saul came…" (9:15 KJV, emphasis added). The literal translation is "God uncovered his ear." The author paints a vivid word-picture of God leaning over Samuel, pushing his hair aside, and whispering to him.

This is the kind of relationship our heavenly Father desires to have with us: intimate, close, and continuous. God is calling us, just as He did Samuel, wanting to participate in our lives and desiring to have us participate in His life. He calls us by name, looking for a response, desiring an opening so that He can come closer.

Why? Because we give Him pleasure. Our companionship, our love, our awareness of His greatness—all these give Him great joy and fulfillment.

The whole purpose for knowing Him, for beginning to experience Him, is to lead us gradually into a life lived next to Him. God is calling you to take hold of His hand and begin a more intimate relationship than you have known before. He wants to start with our moments spent in a structured prayer time and from there slowly begin to spread through the whole of our lives, covering every part with His presence and with His grace.

The best way to really get to know someone is to walk with them through the day: to watch how they respond to situations as they arise, how they treat the different people they meet during the course of the day, what they do with their time, how they work, and how they play. And if in the course of your trailing along beside them you can also talk with them, you begin to gain an understanding of their feelings, of what they think, and of how their character determines their actions. You truly begin to know that person.

God's Call

This is the way God wants you to live your life. He wants you to spend your days beside Him, walking with Him and talking to Him, because as you spend time with Him you will begin to know His character. You will start to see how His character defines His actions. You will begin to understand and share His emotions. You will begin to know Him.

This, more than anything else, is what He wants for you. He is calling you by name, desiring to come closer in relationship than you have ever allowed Him to come. What will be your answer to His call?

> When You said, "Seek My face,"
> my heart said to You, "Your face, Lord, will I seek."
> —Psalm 27:8 NKJV

Reflect

Are there areas you have kept off limits to God?

How you spend your money?
    Your job or your actions there?
        Your way of speaking to people, about people?

Your shopping habits?
    Your reading material, the movies you see?
        Your leisure time?

Do you say to God, "You take care of this, and I'll take care of _____?"

Do you recognize this as your way of keeping control? _____

Study

Read Joshua 22:5.

Do you serve God in the way that Joshua instructs the children of Israel to do in the last part of the verse?

What is the soul of man? _____

In Philippians 3:7-8, Paul talks about the "loss of all things" that he might gain Christ.

What kind of things do you feel Paul is referring to? _____

Could it be his right to his own life? _____

What did Paul say about his travel plans in 1 Corinthians 16:7?
_____

His lifestyle in 2 Corinthians 6:3?_____

What question does Psalm 139:7 ask? _____

What is the answer? (verses 8-12) _____

Where does God's hand lead you? _____

Receiving God's Leadership

Has God been calling you?

Asking to come closer?

Asking to be made part of the "whole" of your life?

Is your fear of a closer relationship with God rooted in your fear of giving over control of certain aspects of your life? _____

Are you ready to talk to God about this today? _____

Pray a prayer of surrender today, giving God control of all your life and asking for His help in answering His call to intimacy.

Prayer of Response

O God,

I know I need to submit all of my life to You, but sometimes it's hard. I'm afraid of what it might mean. Part of me wants to throw myself down in complete surrender and another part holds back, afraid of giving over too much control. Help me, Jesus. You surrendered Your life completely for me; help me to give up my life to You. Take all the parts of my life that I've held back. I submit them all to You.

Amen.

Discussion

What areas of your life do you find difficult to give control of to God?

> *In spiritual issues it is customary for us to put God first, but we tend to think that it is inappropriate and unnecessary to put Him first in the practical, everyday issues of our lives. If we have the idea that we have to put on our "spiritual face" before we can come near to God, then we will never come near to Him.*
> —Oswald Chambers

CHAPTER 19

Trusting

When you begin to walk with God through the ordinary times, "practicing the presence of God," as Brother Lawrence describes it, your experiences with God will still be perplexing at times.

Unless you were born into a perfect environment and a perfect family, there will be problems involved in learning to trust God. It may be difficult for the knowledge we gain of Him through the Word of God and religious instruction to seep down into our emotional life and make a difference in our responses to life's situations and to God Himself.

This is yet another reason for walking with God. Walking with Him gives us the opportunity to know Him, and knowing Him is the only way for us to begin to trust Him.

We stated in the first section that our lack of knowledge and lack of trust in God are two things that prevent us from coming to Him. But as we ask for the Holy Spirit to enable us to come anyway, we will gradually be caught up in a cycle of prayer and slowly unfolding trust in God.

As we pray, we gradually come to know and trust God. When we learn to trust Him we will be more inclined to pray, and this will catch us up into a spiral that leads us closer and closer to Him.

Our knowledge of God and our subsequent ability to trust Him increases as we deal with Him in prayer. When we tentatively start to walk with God in intimate, daily communion, it multiplies even more rapidly.

Walking with God gives us the chance to get to know Him. At the same time, it provides us with the opportunity to receive His assistance. This daily, intimate help gives us a strong foundation of assurance that God cares for us and that He is trustworthy.

However, this isn't always simple. God will have to work through the distortions, fears, insecurities, and wrong concepts about Him that we automatically bring to the relationship. There will be many complexities, many hidden areas that affect God's responses to our prayers, even our intimate daily ones.

God will endeavor to develop our trust in Him, our need for righteousness, our need for deliverance from things we may not even know about yet, and the need to correct our wrong concepts. All of this at the same time He is trying to reveal Himself for who He is and attempting to develop a relationship with us based on mutual trust and love.

This is a tall order. We may have to go through some stormy moments with God. We are not going to understand everything He does, and we are definitely not going to like it all.

However, God is faithful! He will stick with us and He will keep working. Our part is to keep coming to Him and to keep talking! That is what walking with God is all about. Walking with God denotes a constant dialogue with Him. It means when we get to the end of our rope in any situation, we talk to Him about it and tell Him how we feel. With the telling of those feelings to God comes also the release of them to Him.

Looking at many of David's psalms gives us insight into the help he received when he poured out his feelings to God. As you browse through the book of Psalms, you will see how David's prayers reflect his real feelings of anger, bewilderment, or despair. But notice that David's cries of anguish and questioning always end with a statement of faith in God, in spite of the circumstances.

Somehow as you and I, like David, honestly pour out our feelings, it clears the way for God to minister His grace to us so we can be lifted up and given His help, His encouragement, and His strength.

Your willingness to come to Him, your prayer—even though it may be a litany of "I don't like this!" "I don't understand!" and almost always, "Why, God?"—will still open the door of your heart to Him so He can minister His grace to you.

God wants a real relationship with you, one based on honest feelings and open communication.

Trusting

A friend called one day bewailing the circumstances she found herself in. She was using me as a sounding board as she tried to figure out what it all could mean. She and her husband were in the middle of selling their house. The circumstances up to this point couldn't have been more perfect. Everything had gone smoothly and they had been praising God, but that morning their realtor had called and there was a problem. Now she was fluctuating from thoughts of "Maybe we shouldn't sell right now" and "I should have known something would happen; everything had gone so smoothly for a change" to "Why does this kind of thing always have to happen to us?"

I listened to her for a while and made a few suggestions. Then I reminded her to spend some time in prayer before she did anything, talking to God about her concerns, sharing her fears, and then asking for His direction.

She called back about an hour later.

"Well, I talked to God about it. Basically I told Him everything I told you about what I was feeling and what I thought, and I asked Him to help me make sense out of it all. When it got right down to it, my anxiety was caused by the fact that I thought God was behind the sale in the first place and that was why everything was going so smoothly. This glitch destroyed that feeling of assurance, and I was left with the insecurity of not knowing what to do or what God wanted me to do.

"But as I prayed about it, I realized I was putting my trust in the sale itself, and relying on the way the details were all working out as proof that God was directing us and taking care of us. God wants me to get my faith directly from Him, not from the circumstances being perfect."

This is a perfect example of communication with God, based on intimacy, bringing about insight into the reason behind the anxiety. This is how the relationship is supposed to work.

God used my friend's circumstances to teach her a valuable lesson about trusting Him. He also reassured her. And both things happened because she came to Him with her feelings.

Learning to Pray

It seems to take a long time, with lots of interaction and involvement with God through all kinds of situations, for us to come into a smoother, more trusting relationship with our heavenly Father.

Why?

Because we tend to put our trust and our sense of security in everything but God. We find it much easier to trust in the tangible, known aspects of life than in God. We can't see Him or touch Him.

So we put our trust in ourselves and our abilities. We put it in our loved ones. We put it in our job, our bank account, our home. We put it in the status quo of an orderly life. We even try to put our trust in biblical principles in a way that detaches them from God Himself, and we sometimes mistakenly think that "good circumstances" are proof of His direction and blessing.

We base what we know of God on our physical circumstances, but since we live in a world cursed by sin, those circumstances will always be less than perfect.

We cannot know God by looking at circumstances. Oh, we want to! Our whole (carnal) nature is constantly trying to find God everywhere but in a face-to-face encounter, but it just won't work.

Because God's relationship with you and me is the catalyst behind much of what happens in our world, we must begin to realize how important it is that we come to God and learn to trust Him. The relationship can only go as far as our trust of Him will allow.

This is why so much of our prayer life revolves around dealing with God. Until we trust Him we will never choose to walk with Him in intimacy. But we will learn to trust Him in ever-deepening measure as we begin to walk with Him. Like my friend who was looking for knowledge or proof of Him in her circumstances when God was already ahead of her, saying, "No, not that way. Let's do it this way this time." He wanted her to experience a new dimension of trust—trust just in Him.

God has to bring us to the point where our knowledge of Him is based on His actual character and a changed perspective of the world. This new understanding and knowledge only comes about when we actually come to God. We will not understand Him, we will not see things as He sees, and we will not know Him well enough to trust Him until we do.

God would love to be able to do all the things for you that would make you feel loved and cherished. His Father heart delights in giving good things to His children. However, He also wants what is best for us, and He is determined that we will have it, even at the risk of our displeasure with Him.

There will eventually be times as we grow in intimacy with God when He will want to bring a new dimension of trust into our lives. A situation or problem will come our way, a prolonged circumstance in which there is no intervention, and God will want us to put our eyes unswervingly on Him, trusting in Him and walking with Him without the promise, the deliverance, the help, or the answer to the question "Why?"

The trust we need in these times will be ours only as we stay right next to Him. When we are anywhere else, our faith will flounder. When we are walking with God, our gaze can rest constantly on Him, and our trust will be wholly in Him.

Eventually we will find out why God does the things He does. Eventually, as we keep walking with Him, we will turn a corner, the path will straighten and we will look over at God. We will see the little smile there and the expression that says, "Do you understand now?"

Our heart warms within us as once again we realize that God is working things out for our good. Slowly one more chunk of distrust falls from the wall around our heart, and another brick of trust is laid into the foundation of our relationship with God.

Reflect

Do you have a problem with trusting God when answers to prayer take longer than you think they should?

Are you having trouble waiting for deliverance from a problem right now?

Have you been learning to come to God with your feelings?

Learning to Pray

Study

In an earlier lesson we looked at several of David's psalms of complaint. Today, let's look at them again and notice how David finishes these psalms. Read all of each psalm.

Psalm 10. What does verse 14 emphasize? _____

Psalm 13. In verse 5, what is David's response to having to wait for an answer?_____

Psalm 69. Who does David go to in trouble? (verse 13)_____

David came in honesty, expressing his feelings of abandonment, confusion, and hurt, but he then stepped back from the feelings and spoke what he knew about God.

You and I must also learn to distinguish between how we feel and what we know. Your emotions may tell you God isn't helping or doesn't care what is happening to you—but we need to learn to focus on what is true about God.

Read Psalm 74. In what verse does David change from complaint to praise?_____

Maybe you don't know God very well yet, but you can still use the victories you have experienced, the small things you are learning to appreciate, and especially what the Word (truth) tells you about God to acknowledge His goodness, His faithfulness, His mercy, and His lovingkindness.

What are you doing when you make the effort to do this? See Proverbs 3:5b._____

The necessity for praise and worship to God is never more important than during times of confusion and adversity. Learn to make praise, in spite of the circumstances, part of your life every day. It is amazing how your feelings will begin to change to match the truth of what you are saying when you persevere in praising God. It is one of the most powerful tools you have.

Trusting

What does God promise to those who trust Him (make Him their refuge, whose strength is in Him)?

Psalm 5:11 _____

Psalm 32:10 _____

Psalm 40:4 _____

Psalm 84:5 _____

Psalm 112:7-8 _____

Isaiah 57:13 _____

Jeremiah 39:18 _____

What does the New Testament say about those with faith (trust) in God?

Luke 17:6 _____

Romans 4:3 _____

1 John 5:4 _____

Receiving Trust

The book of Habakkuk is a wonderful example to us of a questioning man who came to deal with God about some hard questions. God was very willing to speak to him about it. The book ends with one of the most beautiful prayers of faith in the Bible.

Look up and read Habakkuk 3:17-19. What kind of present day circumstances might this correspond with? _____
_____

Think about whatever circumstances you are now facing that make you question God's goodness/sovereignty. Write out a similar statement of faith using the circumstances you fear in place of those in verse 17.

Though _____,
Yet, I will rejoice in the Lord, I will joy in the God of my salvation.

Discussion

Share with your group a struggle you are having with God and/or your statement of faith.

CHAPTER 20

Struggling in the Stillness

It was Saturday. It was early fall. The weather was gorgeous and Chuck and I had plenty of time to jog and then walk some extra miles, just talking and enjoying the beautiful day before heading home to have breakfast.

We were nearly back to our own street and I was happily talking to Chuck about something that had happened that week, when a bee abruptly flew by the front of my face. I didn't think much about it, but I stopped for a second to glance around and make sure it was gone before continuing my story. When it flew past a second time, I again turned to see where it was, becoming a little more concerned. Bee stings cause me to swell horribly, so anything that buzzes by that closely makes me a little nervous.

Soon it was back again, and for some reason it stayed, darting in and out, close to my head. Instinctively I tried to move away, but it just seemed to become more aggressive. I began to hop around a bit and wave my arms. I knew I probably looked ridiculous, but my only concern was keeping the bee away.

It kept up its incessant circling, so I yelled for Chuck to help. Then I grabbed the jacket I had tied around my shoulders and started swinging it around as a defense against the buzzing, darting bee. Soon I was jumping up and down, turning around to follow the movement of the bee, waving one arm up and down in front of my face, and using the other arm to wave the jacket around. Out of the corner of my eye I could see Chuck standing a few yards away...just watching.

Then, as quickly as it appeared, the bee was gone. I warily turned in a complete circle, making sure it wasn't still close by before I began to calm down. Putting the jacket back around my shoulders, I took a few steps toward Chuck.

"He's gone," I said with relief.

Suddenly the bee flew out of the jacket and onto my face, stinging me on the lip before I frantically reached up to swat it away. The force of my hand stunned it, and when it fell to the ground I angrily began to stomp on it. Then I turned on Chuck, still standing in the same place.

"Why didn't you help me? You knew it was going to sting me. Why did you just stand there?"

The pain hit about that time, along with the realization of what I was going to look like in a few hours, and I started to cry. Chuck came over to hug and comfort me, but I held myself stiffly away from him. I couldn't believe he had just stood there and let it sting me. When I repeated my accusations he tried to reason with me.

"Deb, I couldn't even get close to you. The way you were jumping around and swinging that jacket, you and the bee were moving so quickly I couldn't see where it was to help you. There was nothing I could do. I couldn't get in there." Then, changing his tactics, he started to tease, "You know, you put on quite a show."

I continued to mumble and complain for several minutes as we walked the few blocks home. When we got there I went immediately to a mirror to see if the swelling had started yet. It had.

I sat down in front of the mirror, feeling sorry for myself, trying to accept the inevitability of a face that was going to puff beyond recognition. I thought again about Chuck and my insistence that he could have prevented it. I was beginning to wonder if he could have been any help. My reaction to the bee was the problem in the first place. I knew that bees would not bother me if I didn't bother them or react in a way that stirred them up.

As I sat there looking in the mirror, my thoughts about bees suddenly brought back a mental image of my fourth-grade year and an old, run-down school building.

What was the name of it? I struggled to remember as my thoughts wandered back to that time.

Sycamore School. Yes, that was it. It was an old three-story, turn-of-the-century building that had been the town high school for years. After a new one was built it was scheduled for destruction; however, the growing baby-boom population of the fifties had brought it back into use for a couple of years. During one of those years the district administrators put all of the fourth-grade classes in town over there.

It was an interesting situation. Though the building was three stories, we were only allowed to use the first one (the others were unsafe). There was no playground—just a lot of huge oak trees. And under the eaves of the old structure were hundreds of beehives. Thinking back on it, it's surprising nothing was ever done about them, but I suppose if they could stick us in an unsafe building, they weren't too concerned about bees. As a matter of survival, we had to learn to get along with them.

Since there wasn't a playground, we were always looking for new activities to occupy our recess times. One day some kids came up with the idea of making pets out of the bees. They began to experiment and soon found it was possible to hold them in their hands. If you stayed calm and motionless, you would not get stung. It quickly became the thing to do!

It took me a while to get the courage, but one day I stood very still with my hand outstretched; trying not to be afraid, as a friend gently placed a bee in my open palm. In a few minutes this small but scary insect was crawling all around my hand, and I stood there smiling with a feeling of awe and triumph.

From that point I learned I could move with the bee in hand as long as I kept a sense of calmness, a kind of an inner quietness. The key was learning not to be afraid and to always react with that inner confidence or stillness when other bees would come around.

As I thought about that year, I realized that the occasional bee stings I've had since then, and the subsequent pain and swelling, had gradually destroyed the tenuous hold on the art of being in close proximity to a bee without fear that I had developed during fourth grade. After a time I began again to react to bees with terror and a sort of headlong determination to escape—just as I had that morning.

As I sat staring into the mirror at my rapidly swelling face, I realized that I tend to react the same way when stressful circumstances begin to buzz around my life. At the time, I was dealing with God about some answers to prayer I felt were imperative. Figuratively speaking, I had begun to jump up and down and thrash around, yelling at God to come and help me. I thought my struggling was just a matter of being zealous in prayer so that God could do the thing that needed to be done, but now, as I sat and watched my lip swell, I began to wonder.

When confronted with a situation or desire that arouses strong emotions, we often begin to struggle fiercely to either escape or to bring about the answer to our need. Often we can see what needs to be done, and we may frantically begin to grapple with the situation on our own, calling out for God to help us.

It may seem, in the middle of our inordinate struggling, that He, like Chuck, is just standing by, watching.

In our zeal, we can become angry. He can see our turmoil. Why doesn't He help? Why doesn't He do something?

"Where are You, God? Are You listening?"

Our prayer life at this point begins to take on the same kind of struggling I was involved in with that bee, as we try to encourage God to intervene. The very force of our emotions pushes us to try to dictate to God what must be done and how quickly it needs to happen.

More often than not, when we get into this kind of struggle, we will eventually notice that God is standing aside...waiting.

When we face an area of conflict, we need to have an attitude of trust in addition to our zeal in prayer. When we are fervently praying for God to change something, our praying must come from a heart that is at rest in Him in spite of the situation. We must look to God for the answer and at the same time have that inner sense of confidence in Him. When we don't, God will often wait until we remember, as I needed to remember that fall morning, to stop struggling and be still. He can do nothing to help us until we have ceased struggling and begun to calmly rest in Him again. When in our spirits we resist whatever circumstance has come our way, we are not praying from a heart of trust in God's goodness. When we try by our own effort of will to move God's hand to do something, we are in the way and God cannot work.

At some point in our struggling, we have to stop fighting, stop trying to move God with our fervent pleas, and learn to *be still*. James 5:16 says, "The effectual fervent prayer of a righteous man availeth much" (KJV). So how do we pray with fervency for God to move and change a bad situation, and at the same time have a heart resting in Him?

The answer lies in learning how to keep ourselves in an attitude of trust in our heavenly Father while at the same time endeavoring to receive answers to our prayers. It is not always an easy marriage of two distinct principles given to us by the Word of God. We must learn acceptance at the same time we are seeking God's will in a situation, remembering that "in all things, God works for the good of those who love Him." If He has allowed it into our life, then it must be viewed as part of His overall plan.

God wants us to understand His ways, and He will always be beside us, waiting to help. Unfortunately, He cannot work when we are struggling because usually our struggles are rooted in unbelief. This unbelief causes God to stand aside and wait. When we finally stop struggling and look to Him, He can bring our hearts back into calm acceptance and confidence in His divine care.

I am not saying we should not pray for God to change things and intervene, and I am not saying we shouldn't expect His help. But when we do not receive an immediate answer to prayer, we must be careful not to begin struggling with God.

This kind of turmoil in prayer reflects a heart that is not at rest in God and, again, the underlying cause of our inability to rest in Him is that we do not trust Him. We're always sure we know what is best and often we become like the drowning victim who is thrashing around, desperately trying to save himself when all he has to do is grab hold of the life preserver in the water next to him.

In teaching us about faith, Paul says, "He who comes to God must believe that He is, and that He is a rewarder of those who diligently seek Him" (Hebrews 11:6 NKJV). We must always come to God with belief in who He is, first.

Our faith in God must be rooted in His character so that circumstances or delays in answers to prayer cannot shake our trust. The rest that God promises to believers is synonymous with trust in God:

Come to me, all you who are weary and burdened, and I will give you rest. Take my yoke upon you and learn from me, for I am gentle and humble in heart, and you will find rest for your souls.
—Matthew 11:28-29

There remains then, a Sabbath-rest for the people of God; for anyone who enters God's rest also rests from his own work, just as God did from his.
—Hebrews 4:9-10

This is why God is always working to develop our relationship and to teach us to know Him. Trust in God is another stone in the foundation of the relationship. Our contentment and our joy, which He has promised to us, is directly related to our ability to trust Him and patiently wait upon Him, no matter what the circumstances of our lives may be at any particular time.

Since the relationship between us and God is the most important aspect of our Christian life, He never wants our prayer life or our relationship with Him to become weighted down in struggle. He will patiently wait until we stop our frantic maneuverings and allow Him to lead us gently into the calm, safe waters of His will for us.

Walking with God in intimacy develops the relationship to such a degree that we will always desire His inner rest. His grace is always flowing toward us, enabling us to trust in spite of the circumstances.

However, we will have to keep coming to Him until we know what His heart is in the matter that is disturbing us. We must keep coming until we can accept His will, instead of demanding our own way.

When we keep praying about matters until we are at rest, we can relinquish control to God. Then He can help either by directly intervening in the matter or helping us to

- continue to pray in faith when we have found what His will is in the matter

- relinquish our desire even when we don't know what He will do
- wait in trust (always the hardest)

When our heart is at rest in Him and we are still, God will always show us what needs to be done on our part and enable us to do it.

Reflect

As we are learning to pray we discover an interesting progression. In the beginning our will is in struggle with God's will. We beg. We pout. We demand. We expect God to perform like a magician or shower us with blessings like Father Christmas. We major in instant solutions and manipulative prayers.

As difficult as this time of struggle is, we must never despise it or try to avoid it. It is an essential part of our growing and deepening in things spiritual.
—Richard Foster (*Prayer, Finding the Heart's True Home*)

Are you struggling with God over a matter right now?

Are you demanding your own way or your own timing?

Is God taking too much time to answer your prayers?

Study

What do the following scriptures instruct us to do?

Psalm 27:14 _____

Psalm 37:34 _____

What happens to those who wait? Psalm 40:1-2 _____

Isaiah 64:4 _____

Lamentations 3:24-26 _____

Sometimes, what we know about God is not strong enough to keep our hearts at rest and trusting in Him. At times, the circumstances of our life shout louder than the truths we have learned about God, His character, and His ways.

Whenever we are struggling, there is an aspect of God's character we are forgetting: His sovereignty, His power, His goodness, His mercy…

Psalm 72:18 says "Blessed be the Lord God, the God of Israel, who only does wondrous things."

Think about the word "only." Do you think this statement is true?

What truths about God do you need to remember in order to be at rest?

His sovereignty? Look up…

- Nehemiah 9:6
- 1 Chronicles 29:11-12
- Psalm 33:13-15
- Psalm 103:19
- Daniel 4:2,13,17

His ability to take care of you?

- Psalm 121:5-7
- Isaiah 50:2
- Romans 8:31
- Ephesians 3:20

His desire to do good to you and for you?

- Psalm 100:5
- Psalm 103:17
- Isaiah 43:4

Struggling in the Stillness

Receiving Truth About God

Using the above scriptures, make a verse medley to use when you are struggling with unanswered prayers and are forgetting God's sovereignty over your affairs.

Today, write out and pray a prayer of relinquishment over any matters you have been struggling with God about. Remember to end your prayer with words of faith, choosing one of the scriptures in your verse medley as a basis.

_____

_____

_____

_____

Discussion

Look up Isaiah 25:9 in a King James version, then look it up in an NIV. Notice the word for wait is changed to trust. Do you feel the two words are synonymous?

Share with your group any areas in which you may be struggling with God.

> *God, who is the blessed controller of all things,*
> *the King over all kings and the master of all masters,*
> *the only source of immortality.*
> —1 Timothy 6:15 (Phillips)

CHAPTER 21

Growing Closer

I turned and looked at Matthew in the backseat. "Are you okay?"

"Yeah. It doesn't hurt that much." Then he grinned at me and said, "I can't believe I made the team!"

That was all that mattered to him. He had left the house a few hours before to go to his last in a series of six tryouts for a position on a local soccer team. Now we were rushing him to the hospital.

In what Matt described as a "dazzling jump to head the ball," he had somehow tangled with another player's elbow, ending up with a deep gash above his eye. The coach had brought him home covered in blood, and now we were on our way to the emergency room.

Matt didn't seem to care, though. He was too ecstatic over making the team.

His jubilation gradually became more subdued as we neared the hospital. When we entered the parking lot, he quietly asked, "Is this going to hurt?"

At 17, he's still young enough to ask those kinds of questions.

"Yes." "No." His dad and I answered simultaneously. I gave Chuck a look of exasperation before I continued, "I had stitches as a kid and it didn't hurt. They'll deaden it. You won't feel anything." I didn't see any reason to scare Matt before we even knew what would happen.

Chuck shrugged his shoulders. He had lived through two car wrecks, a motorcycle accident, and Vietnam. Injuries and pain were not something he got very excited about. In fact, his calm during a crisis often irritated me. I viewed it as a lack of compassion.

I put my arm around Matt and gave him a little hug as we entered the emergency room. Chuck went over to the desk to fill out the necessary forms, and Matt and I sat down to wait.

Every few minutes I asked how he was doing, reaching over to rub his back or squeeze his arm. I teased him about his soccer playing to make him laugh, but when he pulled his bandage down and asked me how it looked, I quickly turned away.

Chuck came back about that time, reached over, took Matt's face in his hands and looked it over thoroughly. "It's not so bad." We sat there; watching TV and talking until the nurse came and took Matt back to a room. Chuck and I continued to wait but after about 20 minutes Chuck jumped up and said, "I'm going back there."

I followed him, and we wandered through the halls until I saw Matt's long legs sticking out from behind a curtain. I heard the doctor's voice saying, "You're a tough soccer player. You can handle this..." and I stopped, not certain if I wanted to go any farther.

Chuck hurried on in.

"Do you have a strong stomach?" The doctor greeted him with a question.

"Yeah," Chuck answered as he walked over and stood next to Matt.

I slowly peered around the curtain. My hesitant glance took in the doctor standing over Matt with a needle and Matt's hand gripping Chuck's. Then with reluctant fascination my eyes turned to the bloody gash, made even more vivid in contrast to a white face. My stomach began to roll over, and I turned to rush out.

Back in the waiting room it was another ten minutes before they came out. Neither of them said much, so when we got into the car I began to ask, "How did it go? It wasn't too bad, was it?"

"Yes!" Matt groaned.

"Pretty rough," Chuck agreed. "I guess they don't like to anesthetize that close to the eye. Anyway, it was deep and jagged and they put ten stitches in with no painkillers." He paused and said softly, "I'm glad I was there."

"I'm glad you were, too," I said. Trying to lighten the mood, I turned and grinned at Matt, then laughingly continued, "... so I didn't have to stay."

Chuck caught Matt's eye in the rearview mirror and teasingly commented, "Yeah, I thought he was going to squeeze my hand off."

Matthew smiled wanly, not yet back to his normal sense of humor.

I thought about the incident a lot the next day. I felt bad about not staying in there with Matt. Although I had encouraged him, physically held him, and tried to make jokes to take his mind off it while we were waiting, watching a bloody stitch-up job was just more than I could handle. It was ironic that Chuck, who could seem so unsympathetic at times, was the one who gave Matt his solid, unflinching support during those moments of unavoidable pain.

I thought for a while about the limits each of us has in our capabilities. Because of these limits, neither Chuck nor I can be all things to our children or to each other. Every person has varied and complex needs. Those needs can never be met by a single human being, no matter how special the loved one is.

Then I thought about the distinctive qualities our omnipotent, all-knowing God exhibits to us through the varied moments of our lives. What each of us needs from God is unique, and even within our own lives our needs change from day to day. Yet our heavenly Father can meet them all. He possesses every wondrous quality and knows what we need for Him to be to us at any given time.

As I thought about it, I realized how necessary it was for God to give so many different pictures of Himself throughout the Scriptures and through analogies of Himself in the physical world. God is too vast, too complex, for one physical or biblical analogy to portray. His power, His ability, and His character are too intricate to be described by even a thousand descriptive words and yet He wants to be known.

We spent some time not long ago on a houseboat on Shasta Lake with our children. We were joined by an old friend of mine and her family. The two of us had lived in the area as teenagers and had spent a great deal of time on the lake, so we naturally began to reminisce as different sights pricked our memories.

We showed our children the island to which we had routinely swum until my mother found out and insisted we stop. (It was several hundred yards away from shore, and ski boats raced through constantly.)

Then we pointed to the train trestle underneath a bridge, from which we had jumped after a challenge by another friend. The kids were awed by the distance, but actually the scary part was hoping a train didn't come along before we got out far enough to jump.

I told them about a few of the daring stunts my friend had performed on skis. Gradually I noticed how quiet her kids and mine had become. I thought it was odd, but I soon realized from their puzzled looks that it was probably hard for them to imagine us doing those sorts of things. To them we were both typical, cautious mothers, insisting they eat right, always reminding them not to forget their jackets, and prone to answering requests with "No! It's too dangerous!"

Our children's knowledge of us, like our knowledge of God, was very limited. It was hard for them to know us in any other way than in the role of mother.

In the same way, it is hard for us to know all that God is. We are restricted by our limited experience of Him. Yet He wants us to become gradually aware of the reality of His whole nature. He wants us to know and appreciate Him for who He is.

Our view of God is also limited by our particular personality traits. We tend to endow God with the thinking, the feelings (or lack of them), and the responses that come naturally to us. However, He is so much more varied and complex than we can possibly fathom, and although we will never see God completely in this life (we see through a glass darkly, according to 1 Corinthians 13:12), we can still become much more aware of His various attributes.

God wants us to become aware of who He is. He wants us to participate in a relationship that gradually reveals His wondrous qualities so He can be known, for in knowing Him will come our response of love, admiration, and an awakening desire to be with Him.

God created our world to reveal His power and creativity. He placed mankind into families to enable them to know, through the love of their own children (and parents and brothers and sisters), a portion of His great love for us. Through the magnificent gift of His own Son, He revealed the depth of His love and mercy.

Then by imparting His own Spirit to dwell within us, He made it possible for us to walk with Him daily so He could share our lives. In that intimacy He begins to reveal Himself.

He wants to walk beside us through the "everydays" of our lives—through the momentous events, the hurts and sorrows, the triumphs and joys, and through the mundane and ordinary—so that in each moment beside us, He can reveal Himself. Then we will receive the wonderful benefit of all His qualities: His power and brilliance, His tenderness and love, His righteousness and justice, and His mercy and grace.

When we come to know God, to really begin to understand His ways and glimpse His abilities, feelings, motives, and characteristics, our desire to walk next to Him will grow by leaps and bounds.

As our knowledge and appreciation of God grows through an increasingly close relationship, our awareness of God and His attributes will gradually begin to overshadow the circumstances of our life. Our understanding of God's character becomes part of the foundation of our existence.

As we have seen, in dealing with God we don't just receive answers to prayers, we also receive knowledge of Him. This knowledge begins to create in us a deeper appreciation for who God is. His character becomes known to us in greater measure. We don't just know about Him, we know Him. And that "knowing" of Him, more than anything else, will catch our hearts.

Our response, our love and companionship, is what God was looking for when He created man. As we give Him the opportunity to reveal Himself, we will gradually participate in and enjoy the very thing for which you and I were created: intimacy with God.

Reflect

Do you give God the opportunity to reveal Himself in and through your circumstances and prayers?

Is your prayer life becoming more about relationship and being with God than before?

> *Think about the last thing you prayed about—were you devoted to your desire or to God? Was your determination to get some gift of the Spirit for yourself or to get to God? "For your Father knows the*

things you have need of before you ask Him" (Matthew 6:8). The reason for asking is so you may get to know God better. "Delight yourself also in the Lord, and He shall give you the desires of your heart" (Psalm 37:4). We should keep praying to get a perfect understanding of God Himself.

—Oswald Chambers

Study

Why were the Israelites told they needed a new heart? Jeremiah 24:7

_____

Why did Jesus come to the earth? 1 John 5:20 _____

For what did Paul count all things loss? Philippians 3:8-12

_____

What did he press on to receive? verse 12 _____

What is Jesus' goal? (go back to verse 10) _____

In Hosea 6:3, what does God promise to do when we pursue knowledge of Him? _____

_____

Receiving New Knowledge of God

Read Hosea 11:1-4.

God's relationship with Israel (Ephraim) is God's analogy of His relationship with you and me, and His dealing with them is a picture of His dealing with us.

What picture of God do these verses give? _____

Read this section again slowly, reflecting on the image of God it gives. Now put yourself in the picture...

> your heavenly Father holding you up as you learn to walk...
>   taking your hands when you stumble...
>   and bending down to feed you as a mother feeds her child.

Read Isaiah 49:15-16. Meditate on these words and receive them as God's words to you today.

Prayer of Response

Respond to God's love for you by asking Him to help you become a seeker: one who desires to know Him intimately.

Discussion

What are some of the earthly relationships God uses to reveal His relationship with us?

Isaiah 63:16 _____

Isaiah 54:5 _____

John 15:14 _____

John 10:11-15 _____

Hebrews 2:10-11 _____

Isaiah 62:5b _____

Think about those relationships. What aspect of each one (if they were perfect) portrays God's relationship to us?

WORKING WITH GOD

My yoke is easy and my burden is light.
—Matthew 11:30

CHAPTER 22

Not Just My Own Needs

I thought she was going to talk forever!" I muttered as my friend and I finally escaped from one of her neighbors. We walked together once a week and used the time to talk and catch up on each other's activities.

But that morning one of my friend's neighbors had been outside and had waved us down to talk. I didn't mind at first. I was introduced and politely chatted also for a few minutes, but I soon realized the woman was going to keep talking as long as we would listen. My friend is a people person and dearly loved for her friendly manner and compassionate listening skills.

"She is the perfect target for someone like this," I thought as we stood there.

As time went on, I mentally rolled my eyes and tried to think of a way to excuse us so we could continue. I didn't know this woman, and I wanted to leave. It wasn't long until, with an excuse that was all too transparent, I broke in and dragged Marci away.

The minister introduced the next baptismal candidate, briefly telling a little about the man and his recent conversion. *"He looks familiar,"* I thought. *"Do I know him?"*

As I listened to the minister, I kept trying to place the man. *"Ohhhh, that's the man who irritated me with his rude, out-of-place behavior a few weeks ago."*

Now, as I realized he had been new to our church at the time, I felt bad about my harsh, judgmental attitude toward his participation in our church service. When will I ever learn, I thought. Once again I regretted my quick and critical assessments of people and situations.

I've mentioned these two recent incidents (sometimes I wonder if God will ever get me all cleaned up) because I want to be sure you understand the kind of character we're dealing with before I share with you about my ventures into the realm of intercession.

I am not, by nature, a compassionate person. Oh, there is a part of me that is sensitive to hurting people, but there is also a great deal of self-centered, unconcerned, he-made-his-own-bed-now-let-him-lie-in-it philosophy. Therefore, when God uses me to intercede for someone with real compassion and concern, I know it is the work of the Holy Spirit. I just don't have that kind of nature on my own. It still amazes me that God can use me in this area.

I hesitate to use the word "intercessor" to describe myself, just as I hesitate to use any personal examples of intercessory prayer, because I am so aware of my lack in this area. What I have learned has been because of God's great forbearance with my personal failings and His unaccountable determination to teach me in spite of the self-centered and uncaring response of my basic nature to the needs of the world around me.

I am a surprising mix of sensitivity to some hurts (usually my own) and callous indifference to others. Like everyone else, I find it much easier to pray over my own needs and desires than for those of others.

Can God really take people like me and you and expect us to intercede with real compassion and love for the world around us?

I was glancing at a magazine the other day, and as I was leafing through it I came upon a map of the world. Every continent was pictured, with the names of each country. I don't remember why it was in there, an advertisement of some kind probably, but it caught my attention. Suddenly I started to cry.

It was a odd reaction. A map, to me, has always evoked feelings of adventure and a desire to travel. Now my response was to think of the desperate need for the gospel to be preached in so many countries.

Not Just My Own Needs

I was startled at my response, but as I thought about it, it wasn't hard to find the reason behind my reaction. A friend of mine had given me a world prayer diary a few years before, and I had become very excited about this new systematic way to pray over the world and unreached people-groups. The diary contains maps of each continent and general information about each country, and then gives a short description of any religious activity in the various places. It systematically lists cities and nations, and also describes various people-groups that are still unreached with the gospel message.

In the first few months my attempts to use the prayer diary left me feeling discouraged and guilty. Since a part of me really wanted to continue, I began to ask God to help me be more disciplined in using it. Gradually I became involved with it in a way that amazed me.

Somehow God took the little desire I did have to intercede for missionary endeavors and began to build on it. For the last several years I have been praying daily for the various countries and peoples of the world.

It is really only minutes out of each day, sometimes more, sometimes less, which I give to this particular "work" of prayer, but it is slowly making a difference in my own outlook and response to the world and its problems.

I am beginning to see events in the world in the light of their effect on the preaching of the gospel of Christ. I read the paper and listen to world news with a totally different perspective.

The civil war in Liberia grieved me as I read about hundreds being killed because I knew many had not heard the gospel. The horrors of Rwanda drove me to ask God to intervene. I began to see the working of Satan in many of those kinds of events. I began to pray as I read about them, binding the forces of darkness and asking for God to move to bring about a change.

I began to pray for our own country with the thought of opportunities to reach out to the world with the gospel. I began to ask God to raise up young men and women to be missionaries. And now, to my surprise, a glimpse of a map of the world brings tears of compassion for the lost.

Learning to Pray

I wish I could say that I was responsible for this change in outlook, but I really wasn't. I wish I could say it happened because I was becoming such a wonderful person, but that isn't true, either. I still yell at my kids at times, and I still have trouble keeping my impatience under control when I get a slow checker at the supermarket. God is still working in me.

No, the reason for my change in outlook and my venture into intercession isn't that I've suddenly become a spiritual giant, but rather because God has been drawing me to begin to spend time working with Him in praying for His will to be done.

Intercession can be hard work, but God is amazingly gentle in what He asks of us, and He is so faithful to reward us with rest and refreshing when we have learned to pray in response to His burdens and His timing. His yoke truly is easy and His burden really is light.

God has much to do, much He wants to do, and much He can do when He has a child committed to walking beside Him and sharing the burden of His heart.

When God delivered the Israelites from Egypt and led them into the Promised Land, they were given work to do. God gave them the land of Canaan. It was theirs to possess, but it entailed the work of ridding the country of the enemies of God.

God promised to go before them and behind them, but they had a part to play in the possession of the land. He wanted them to clear the land of the heathen tribes, tear down their altars, and destroy their images and gods. God wanted a people, a country, set apart for Him and ready to do His will.

You and I, like the Israelites, have been set apart. We have been chosen, but along with the privileges of being children of God comes work to do. Some of that work lies within the prayer life of every Christian.

Through prayer, you and I participate in bringing about God's will on earth. Although God uses each of us in different capacities, we all have one job in common: intercession.

Not Just My Own Needs

Through intercessory prayer, you and I work with God. We pray His will into our own lives, into our family and friends' lives, into our church, and into a lost and dying world. God has ordained prayer as the first step in accomplishing His will on earth:

> Our Father who art in heaven,
> hallowed be thy name.
> Thy kingdom come,
> Thy will be done!

About ten years ago we were on a snow skiing trip in a resort area. It was a holiday weekend, all the restaurants were crowded, and we were waiting in the lounge area until we could get a table for dinner. As we sat waiting, I watched a young, seductively dressed woman enter the restaurant and slowly scan the entire room before walking over to join a couple of men seated at the bar.

I continued to watch her as she sat next to them and leaned over to talk animatedly. She gestured and flirted, but the men remained unresponsive to her overtures. I watched her as she kept trying to elicit a favorable response from the two men; she seemed completely unaware of the fact that they were regarding her with open contempt. My initial reaction of scorn changed to sadness and pity as I realized she was probably on drugs and trying to get money to buy more.

I pointed her out to Chuck, but about that time our name was called for dinner and I forgot about her until a few days later.

We were back home, and I was in my family room. I had just finished reading a few chapters in the Bible and had begun to pray. Suddenly, into the middle of my planned list of things to pray about that morning came a picture of the girl in the restaurant. A rushing wave of grief swept across my being, and I started to cry as compassion filled me. Immediately, without plan, prayers for her literally poured from deep inside me.

I began to ask God to intervene in her life and save her. I prayed for the chains of deception and sin, so evident in her life, to be broken. I asked the Holy Spirit to prepare her heart to receive the gospel of Jesus Christ, and then I asked God to send people into her life to be witnesses to the love of Christ.

After a while the storm of intercession subsided, and I went on to pray for other matters. But for the next few days, the burden to intercede for her settled over me again and again when I knelt down to pray. Throughout the day my thoughts went back to the girl in the restaurant, and I found myself whispering little prayers for her. This lasted for about a week. Then, just as suddenly as it came, the burden lifted.

Now, all these years later, something will occasionally remind me of the incident and of my prayers for her, and I'll wonder about that young woman. I know I'll never meet her. I wouldn't know her if I did. I don't know her name. I don't remember anything about her—the color of her hair or eyes, her height, any distinguishing characteristics. But somehow I know her, and I think I will know her in heaven.

You see, I believe God answered my prayers for her because He laid the assignment of prayer on my heart. I believe God saw a heart that would respond to Him and wanted to intersect that young woman's life and save her. Before His Holy Spirit could complete the work, however, someone had to pray.

And someone has to pray before God can finish His work in countless lives today. Someone has to pray before God can reach down and deliver souls from darkness. Someone has to pray before God can bring healing to the sick. Someone has to pray before God can bring good from seemingly impossible situations. Someone has to pray before God can break the strongholds of sin and deception in the world today.

This is the work that God calls you and I to do. This is how you and I join Him in labor as we pray for His will on earth.

And the rewards?

Our women's group at church had a dinner meeting the other night, and I stayed to help clean up. I always do. Not because I love to work, but because that hour of working together with friends is usually a lot of fun. Different women stay to help at different times, and it is an opportunity to get to know them, plus a chance to spend time with old friends.

We take turns scrubbing pots and pans and wait on the old dishwasher to get through another cycle. We open every drawer looking for the garbage bags, since we can never seem to remember where they're kept. We argue over who dried the forks and knives last time and divide up the tablecloths to take home and wash. We put a zillion things away, and it is work, but the sharing and companionship of the other women makes it fun.

Intercession is work too, but when we cooperate with the Holy Spirit, we will find that the work we do will bring us a great deal of pleasure, because we are doing it with God. We begin to know Him in yet another way as we take on the concerns of His heart.

When we allow the Holy Spirit to pray the will of our Father through us, taking the time to find His heart's desire when we come to pray, we will begin to experience a depth and fulfillment unlike any other experience we might have in the Lord.

There is fellowship with the Holy Spirit and an ever-deepening knowledge of how God perceives the world around us, both the far corners of the world and the situations and people close to us. There is a new intimacy with our heavenly Father as He allows us to come even closer to His heart, as we are allowed a glimpse into His plans and purposes, and as we are made aware of His own anguish and grief over the lost, the wounded, the spiritually blind and needy. Then there is the excitement as we realize the change that He will bring when we pray with Him for His will to be done, and we realize we are part of the victory.

Working with God in intercession gives us a sense of unity and singleness of purpose. It brings joy as we realize we are joined together with God in pursuit of the good that is always behind His will, and it brings satisfaction and a sense of accomplishment unequaled by anything else we will ever do.

Because all begins with God, He is faithful to begin His work by drawing us into His presence and burdening our hearts to pray.

We must respond, however, by making ourselves available to pray, by answering His call to prayer, and by praying His will. Then He is free to move upon the earth, accomplishing His good in our lives, sending forth His angels to intervene and work, directing His Spirit to draw men and women to Christ, and enabling you and me to carry out His will.

God has ordained prayer as His way to establish and maintain a relationship with us, and it is His desire to involve you and me in yet one more aspect of a close union: working together toward a common goal. It is in this working union that we will come to know and understand the heart of God in a way that is not possible through any other kind of communication we have with Him. We will literally begin to know His heart's desire—His concerns, His purposes, and His intentions—as we join Him by praying for His will to be done.

Prayer does not enable us to do a greater work for God.
Prayer is a greater work for God.
—Thomas Chalmers (1780-1847)

Reflect

Are you ready to join with our Lord Jesus in intercession?

      Do you feel unable?
           unwilling?

Do you doubt your ability to make intercession a regular part of your prayer life?

Study

What truths from our study in chapters 4 and 5 will help us as we consider this next step in prayer?

Isaiah 40:29 _____

2 Corinthians 12:9_____

Philippians 4:13_____

1 Thessalonians 5:23-24_____

Not Just My Own Needs

Choose one and write it out in your own words, using whatever phrase describes what you need in order to become an intercessor.

_____

_____

_____

What does Galatians 3:26 tell us we are? _____

What has happened to us as sons? Gal. 4:6? _____

_____

In 1 Peter 2:5, how are you and I described? _____

What are we promised in John 16:23? _____

Receiving a New Heart for Intercession

Consider what work of intercession you can begin to make a part of your regular prayer time. What kinds of things are you concerned about? Evangelism, missions, church ministries, young people, social problems, salvation for your friends, neighbors, coworkers?

Ask Jesus to help you begin to make regular intercession for the needs of others more a part of your life.

Prayer of Response

Dear Jesus,

I want to join You in the work of intercession. I ask You to give me a desire to pray for others and I ask that You would give me a specific work of intercession. I want to pray for the things that concern You. Help me to know Your heart and Your desires so I can pray Your will.

I want to begin today to be available to you for the work of intercession.

Amen.

Discussion

Share what kind of intercession you would like to be involved in. As a group, take on a prayer project* that you will all pray about in the upcoming weeks.

> *A sign of friendship with God is to keep asking Him to share with us the concerns closest to His heart.*
> —Joy Dawson

*Ideas for Prayer Projects

Adopt a country to pray for. Gather information about the country (the internet is a great resource). Find out about missionaries who are already there. Or pray for a country that is not open to the gospel.

Use your newspaper as a catalyst to pray for war-torn countries or needs in your own country.

Adopt an unreached people group to pray for.

Try a prayer walk through your neighborhood, praying for each household. Ask God to draw them to Jesus, to send Christians into their lives to witness, to remove the darkness and unbelief that keeps them from knowing Christ, to prepare their hearts to be open to the gospel...

Pray for a different emphasis each day of the week (for example, missions one day, your church another day, your country and those in government, salvation for those in your community, your neighborhood).

Gather information regarding the needs you pray about. It helps you to be specific and gives a basis for prayer.

CHAPTER 23

Don't Stop Now

I bought my son an electric razor yesterday. I saw an advertisement for one on sale in the morning paper, got in the car, maneuvered through the already heavy traffic and crowds out shopping for Christmas, bought it, brought it home, and gave it to him—even though I had been telling him if he wanted one he would have to wait until Christmas.

But I wasn't very gracious when I gave it to him. I just said, "Here. Happy Wednesday, but that is one less Christmas present under the tree."

Why? Because I was sick and tired of having him nag me about it. He had become convinced, after using a friend's, that an electric shaver wouldn't irritate his skin as much as a razor. He had begun to relentlessly badger me to buy him one, bringing it into every conversation no matter how unrelated the subject was.

I told him that a onetime use didn't prove anything; Chuck told him that electric shavers could be more irritating to sensitive skin. I repeatedly said that if he wanted it, he would have to wait until Christmas, but eventually I just got tired of hearing about it and went out and got one for him.

I thought about my response as I read Jesus' parables about the importunate neighbor in Luke 11 and the persistent widow in Luke 18. In the first story, Luke tells about the man who is already in bed when his friend comes and knocks on the door, asking for a loaf of bread to feed a late visitor. The parable says that although the man may not get up and give the bread because his friend is asking, yet because of his importunity (persistence) he will get up and give him as much as he needs. The parable in Luke 18 is about a widow who continues to ask a judge to avenge her until he agrees, saying, "Lest by her continual coming she weary me" (v. 5 KJV).

I had over the course of a few weeks become very willing to give my son an electric shaver because, frankly, he had begun to weary me.

Do you think that is how God is with us? Is that how importunity works? These parables tell us that persistence pays off, so does it all boil down to badgering God until we've worn Him down or until we've finally prayed whatever arbitrary quota of words are needed for that particular request? Is this what the work of prayer is all about?

Because of the abundant evidence given both in Scripture and experience that prayer changes things, it is sometimes tempting to reduce prayer into a formula for getting something from God.

We decide to pray repeatedly for something we want God to do, feeling that the more prayer offered, the more likely God will do what we ask. But we must always be careful to keep prayer within the framework of the relationship we have with God, so that our prayers are not simply an attempt to overwhelm Him with a lot of words, and by that earn an answer.

Jesus was careful to balance His teaching about importunity with the Scripture in Matthew 6:7: "But when ye pray, use not vain repetitions, as the heathen do: for they think that they shall be heard for their much speaking" (KJV).

Sometimes we have the idea that we can influence God by our "much speaking" and make Him interested in us, good to us, and kindly disposed to us so He'll give us what we want. We think we can "earn" an answer by praying persistently. This stems from the age-old desire of mankind to try to reach God by his own merits. That kind of thinking is the basis for many religions but has no place in Christianity, which is based entirely on the grace of God and the work of Jesus Christ. Our part is always to receive; never to earn—not even by praying.

Earning an answer by "doing" something, even if what we are "doing" is prayer, is not the philosophy behind Christ's teaching on importunity. We cannot earn answers to prayer because we've prayed long enough or hard enough. Our prayers do not make God interested in us or good to us. He already is. Our prayers do not make God feel differently about us. He already loves us more than we can imagine and continuously keeps what is best for us in mind.

Our prayers are for the express purpose of opening ourselves up to Him. They are not about getting something from Him by mechanically fulfilling an arbitrary amount of prayer, but rather about opening ourselves, our needs, and the needs of others to His great love.

Prayer's value lies in the fact that as we talk to God a connection is made, interaction takes place, and relationship happens. When our prayers are just words we say to get something, we've reduced it to yet another ritual or form of religion. When the words are spoken without thought or emotion, the prayer has no real meaning or purpose because we have not truly made a connection with God.

But as our whole self—our mind, our will, and our emotions—participates in the prayer process, a connection will come about.

First and foremost, prayer is a way to connect us to God, and this is one of the reasons for importunity in prayer. Remember, God's chief goal isn't just to save all the lost in the world; it is also for you to know Him intimately.

This is why James taught us that "the effectual fervent prayer of a righteous man availeth much" (James 5:16 KJV).

The words "effectual fervent" are translated from one Greek word, *energeo*. This word is translated in other Scriptures as "work" or "to work in." This puts an interesting light on these often-quoted words showing us that the prayers of a righteous man are powerful and persuasive.

Remember that our righteousness is derived from our faith, our trust and belief in God. So one aspect of having powerful prayers is that we believe God is listening and desires to answer our prayers. This steadily growing faith in God comes about as we learn to know God in and through our prayer relationship with Him.

But it is the *energeo* of praying that we need to think about. This Scripture seems to be telling us that the kind of prayer that avails much is the prayer of energy or work. Prayers that are prayed with energy influence God.

What does that mean? That the person with the most emotion or fervor in prayer has a greater chance of being answered?

Well...yes.

This really shouldn't surprise us in light of what we have already learned about prayer and God's attitude toward us.

If prayer is the foundation and the essence of our relationship with God, then it is reasonable to assume that God is more apt to listen with greater concern and response when our emotions and energy are involved in our prayers to Him.

When we are interested in, concerned about, or deeply desirous of the things we talk to Him about, our emotions prompt His emotions.

Because He loves and cares about us, the things we care about deeply will bring about an emotional response in Him, causing Him to care deeply along with us. Emotion evokes emotion.

We know this is true in our own lives. When a speaker reveals genuine emotion, we respond in kind. When someone we love calls us with happy news, we become happy, too. When someone dear to us is suffering, we suffer also. When a friend is anxious, we feel anxious. We identify with others' feelings, especially when it is someone we care about.

In the same way, God identifies with our feelings. Because of His great love for us, He takes on our emotions as we come to Him. Our stirred passions give energy (energeo) to our prayers, and God's heart is engaged in much greater measure than it would be by any mindless litany of words.

Fervency in prayer doesn't make God love us more, and it can't be used to get something from God, but rather it is, or should be, a reflection of real emotions that emanate from our innermost being regarding the things we are praying about.

There is something about our emotions that can prompt God to act. Perhaps it is because true emotions can't be easily counterfeited; we can't work them up. Effective prayer keeps us from doing as the pagans do, reducing prayer to a mindless ritual, a recital of needs or wishes, in the hopes that our many words will earn an answer. It keeps us from "working" for answers to prayer without the opening of ourselves and our emotions to God in a way that brings about a true connection between us.

Our zeal in prayer and in asking from God prompts a response. It brings us into His presence often. It connects us to Him and allows for a continual interchange of ideas and thoughts. But just as important, it allows for an interchange of feelings and emotions. Eventually we begin to know what God is feeling and what is on His heart, and our prayers begin to be a reflection of that.

A psychologist will tell you that there are five levels of communication between people. Communication starts with cliches and moves to interchanges of facts and information, followed by ideas and judgments, and then eventually a sharing of feelings. But the peak level of communication is when two people share in such a way that each is aware of the other's feelings at the moment and is completely in tune with the other person. That is intimacy.

The same is true for you and me in our relationship with God the Father. In order for there to be any real intimacy, there must be sharing on a deeper level than just a rote recital of needs or a time of perfunctory prayer. We vitally need times of deeper contact with our heavenly Father; it is essential to the health of our relationship.

This is why God desires "fervent" prayer. Fervency, or zeal, involves emotions, and real emotions bring about vulnerability. Stirred emotions bring an opening within us that enables another person a glimpse into who we really are. But it gives God much more than that; it gives Him the opportunity to come into yet another area of our life.

This is the reason God has set aside fervent effectual prayer as special to Him and "availing much," so that even in "working" with God in prayer we will be connected to Him in an intimate way.

But where does the emotion or "fervor" come from in intercession? It may be easy to express emotion in our prayers when we are praying for something dear to our heart, but when our prayers are for other people—missions, our church, distant lands, or neighbors who need Jesus—where do we get the emotion and fervor needed to pray with effectiveness?

Our own emotions can only carry us so far in praying for the needs around us. Our feelings of compassion arise readily in response to tragedy or sadness. We want to do something. Often the only thing we can do is pray, and that is the right response. But our emotions are easily used up and primarily self-centered. Sometime during the growth of our prayer relationship we will need to allow the emotions of the Holy

Spirit to flow through us, enabling us to pray with consistency and fervor and importunity.

Being importunate in prayer is praying with honesty realness and with emotion. It is this fervor, this genuine emotion expressed and shared with our heavenly Father, that is so pleasing to Him, and it is this ingredient in prayer that enables us to pray prayers that avail much. We will gradually learn that even though our own emotions cannot sustain fervent prayer, the Holy Spirit will always enable us to pray with fervor and importunity until the will of God is accomplished.

Reflect

> The earnest (heartfelt, continued) prayer of a righteous man makes tremendous power available—dynamic in its working.
> —James 5:16 (AMP)

Study

Look up James 5:16 in different translations and write down some of the words used to describe a righteous man's prayers._____

What kinds of actions seem to be part of earnest prayer?

Nehemiah 1:4_____

Hebrews 5:7_____

Romans 8:26_____

Colossians 4:12_____

Hebrews 5:7_____

Read Luke 11:1-13.

What are the three separate teachings about prayer in this section of scripture? _____

_____

_____

Do you feel this parable is "comparing" God to the unjust judge or "contrasting?"_____

What term is used to describe God?_____

Underline the phrase "how much more."

Contrast the fervent, persistent prayer spoken of in James 5:16 with the kind of praying Paul alludes to in Romans 1:9, Ephesians 1:16, Philemon 4, and 1 Thessalonians 1:2. What words does he use that may describe the kinds of prayers he prayed for those he was writing to?

_____

This phrase seems to describe the action of bringing someone's name up to God, but not in a lengthy way. There seems to be a time for both kinds of praying: making mention of someone in prayer and prayers that are persistent and impassioned.

Receiving New Fervency in Prayer

In the second section of the book, we talked about becoming involved with God in prayer as a way to open us up to Him. Do you see that persistence and fervent prayer is a part of that process?

Look again at the passage in Luke 11. Read verse 9 and then look up Matthew 7:7. If you have an Amplified Bible, look it up in that translation.

A better reading of this scripture says, "Keep on asking, keep on seeking, keep on knocking…"

Jesus knew the necessity of having his disciples (including you and me) keep coming back again and again, so the relationship could be built. Part of that relationship-building is through sharing in concerns dear to His heart and yours.

Prayer of Response

Dear Jesus,

Help me to learn the principles of fervent, persistent prayer and learn how to share Your emotions for the needs of the world around me. I don't want to try to earn an answer, but I understand persistence is sometimes needed for Your will to be done.

Amen.

Discussion

Have you ever felt you were trying to "pray enough" to receive an answer from God?

Prayer is not overcoming God's reluctance;
it is laying hold of His highest willingness.
  —Archbishop Richard Chenevix Trench (1895-1979)

CHAPTER 24

New Strength for Prayer

"I don't think His yoke is so easy or His burden light," a friend confided to me. "This year, I've been involved with people and situations that required real intercession and, frankly, I ended the year exhausted by it all!"

Then she repeated, "I'm just not sure His yoke is all that easy."

It was a thought-provoking observation from someone who really was trying to pray so that God could make a difference in her world. It was also interesting to me personally because I was trying to finish this book on prayer in which that verse is the central theme.

"Father," I prayed the next morning, "show me the answer to this paradox. Why does my friend think her concerned praying over situations is 'almost too exhausting to be involved in'?"

I wasn't sure why my friend was having difficulties. I thought prayer was wearisome at times too, but those feelings didn't usually last beyond the next prayer time and usually involved my inability to trust God in some way. I was pretty sure the answer for my friend, however, was somehow related to her understanding of the role of the Holy Spirit in intercessory prayer.

Perhaps my friend was not using the help that God had given her in the person of the Holy Spirit.

If we are to be effective in the area of intercession, and if we are going to be able to labor with God without the work becoming a hardship, then we will have to learn how the Holy Spirit works through us to accomplish the intercession this world needs.

Not all intercessory prayer is hard work, but it can be. There is work to be done, there is physical energy to be expended when we are part of God's kingdom. Paul did say of his work for the church and the kingdom of God: "To this end I labor, struggling with all his energy, which so powerfully works in me" (Colossians 1:29). However, if we focus on the word "struggling" in that Scripture, we'll miss the whole point, which is revealed in the words "with all His energy, which so powerfully works in me."

Paul is referring to the Holy Spirit. He is reminding us that the Holy Spirit is the catalyst and the energy behind anything we do for the kingdom of God.

In the area of intercession, it is the job of the Holy Spirit to point out specific prayer needs and to draw us to pray. But He does more than that. He gives us the compassion we need in order to pray fervently as He burdens us to pray and literally prays the will of the Father through us.

Our part is to willingly respond and make ourselves available. And although there may be times of physical and mental exhaustion during times of intense intercession, God is faithful to reward us with rest and refreshing. The Holy Spirit knows our limitations and He will never ask too much of us.

Long-distance runners know how to pace themselves so they can finish the race. The Holy Spirit, our guide in prayer, knows how to pace us also. That is why we must learn to work with God in submission to the Holy Spirit's direction. We need to allow Him to lead us in and out of times of intercession, and we need to learn to accept the rewards and rely on the refreshing He offers.

I have found that the tiredness I feel after spending time and exertion in intercession is always the good tiredness you feel after a job well done. If you are feeling so exhausted that you question its worth, perhaps you need to examine how you are praying. Perhaps you are taking on concerns that the Lord has not asked you to carry. Maybe you need to allow the Holy Spirit to reveal what is going on that perhaps is unnecessary.

Perhaps you've turned your desire to pray for someone or something into a legalistic duty instead of bringing that need to God and allowing the Holy Spirit to help you pray.

To better understand how the Holy Spirit helps us in prayer we need to examine "prayer burdens"; what they are and what they are not.

The word "burden" is often used to refer to a weight or hardship, but that is not what is meant by a burden to pray. Another meaning for the word "burden" is "something often repeated or much dwelt upon: recurring: the principle idea." This is exactly what a prayer burden is: a recurring theme in our prayers given to us by God. It is something He wants us to pray about and keep praying about until we see the answer or until He no longer puts the concern to pray over it into our hearts. It is like a charge given to us by God to pray over a matter again and again. You might also consider a prayer burden a prayer assignment.

Many things concern us, but not everything is a prayer assignment from God. We must learn to recognize the difference.

First, *a prayer assignment is not worry.*

Unlike worry, a prayer assignment focuses on God. It draws our hearts toward Him for help, and it carries with it inherent faith.

A prayer assignment is God-centered. When our anguish is centered on the problem, the circumstance, or a sense of responsibility, it is not a God-given burden. Obviously, anything that worries us or causes concern is to be brought to God in prayer, but when we have truly prayed over a matter our worry should begin to change to trust.

Prayer assignments are not negative emotions or attitudes such as anxiety or despair. Sometimes we confuse our own out-of-control emotions with a prayer assignment from God. Obviously, we are to pray during any troublesome situation until we can release our emotions to God, but negative emotions will not necessarily draw you to pray. A prayer assignment will. Negative emotions and worry focus on the problem. A prayer assignment will automatically focus upon God.

There is, of course, an element of concern in an assignment given by God, but the concern looks to God and realizes God must help and God wants to help.

A prayer assignment is not a weight of responsibility for someone or something. It is not something given to us to carry around with a sense of obligation. We must cultivate an attitude of "my part is simply to obey the Spirit's direction. The rest is up to God." A prayer assignment also does not make us responsible for the answer to our prayers. God may use you in some way other than prayer, and He may not.

We must also learn to carry only the prayer burdens God gives and only for the time He gives them. We must guard against the tendency of some overly responsible individuals to carry people and situations in a way God never intended. For example, we may decide to spend such and such a time praying for a situation without any thought to finding the will of the Spirit in the matter.

When we pray because we feel responsible instead of as a response to the Holy Spirit's direction, then the feelings of responsibility have overshadowed our awareness of God working through us and in the lives of the people for whom we are praying. At that point, prayer will become wearisome in a way it was never meant to be.

Prayer assignments cannot be sustained by our own compassion. At the end of choir practice recently we took a few minutes to share prayer needs before closing in prayer. We normally do this, but that night some of the needs were so gripping—a young mother in our church with cancer; a boy, the son of one of our choir members, with a serious and painful disease; a teenager, a friend of my children, facing brain surgery for an aneurysm. Serious business!

I found myself whispering softly, "Father, give me Your prayer assignments for these needs during my quiet time in the morning. Help me to pray Your will!" For even though my emotions were touched during the time of sharing and prayer after choir, I knew that I could easily lose that feeling of urgency to pray. To really do any serious work in prayer, I would need the Holy Spirit's help to quicken my spirit to pray.

During the years of my personal prayer odyssey, my whispered prayer to the Holy Spirit for help has changed from "Draw me to pray" to "Draw me to pray the will of my Father."

That doesn't mean I don't tell God about all those things which concern me. It just means that I want to also spend time praying what is on God's heart.

Not everything that we pray about will arouse emotions and come from a burden to pray. It is important, however, that we spend time with God each day, allowing Him to burden our hearts to pray over needs that are on His heart. We need to be available to the Holy Spirit and watchful for His prompting to pray about matters.

My praying over the world and unreached people-groups came out of simple desire rather than any explicit feeling of purpose or calling. I can see now, however, that God was behind that desire.

As I began, it was simply a matter of reading the material my friend had given me and praying each day for the people group and city or country for that particular day. Gradually, however, I noticed that sometimes it was easier to pray over a particular people or place. I was given compassion for them as I prayed, and this activated my emotions and gave fervency to my prayers. There were times when I was so heavily burdened to pray that my intercession came with groans that words cannot express just like Paul described in Romans 8:26.

I was learning to be available for God's assignments as I routinely prayed for the people and places listed in my prayer diary. This is the way we are to come to prayer each day, *with an outward intent to pray over specific needs and, at the same time, an inward searching for the mind of the Spirit and His direction in prayer.*

As we do this, we will find that the Holy Spirit is always faithful to help us to pray as we should, laying those things that God wants us most to pray about on our heart. This may not always mean intercession for people far away. God will also tell us how to pray specifically for ourselves and our family. It is wonderful to be able to trust Him to bring to the forefront those things that should be prayed about and then to show us how to pray.

A prayer assignment is not faithless. When a prayer assignment is from God, it carries with it hope and faith because we are praying God's will.

An assignment from God *is always directed toward a specific end*—something or someone He wants to change, a need He wants to fill, a work He wants to do. When God burdens our hearts to pray, He intends to do something about the thing for which He has burdened us.

If He has burdened you for someone who is lost, He intends to work in their life to draw them to salvation.

If He has burdened you to pray for someone with a problem, He wants to take care of that problem.

If it is a burden about a change needed in someone's life, He intends to deal with them about that change.

If it is a burden for a group of people who have not received the gospel, it means He is preparing hearts and orchestrating events to bring a witness of Christ.

An assignment to pray that comes directly from the Holy Spirit is a cause for faith to rise in our hearts. It means God wants to do something. It means He is simply waiting for the prayers to be uttered so that He can respond. It means He wants to work. He wants to bring about change. He wants to bring deliverance and help.

Our job is to allow the Holy Spirit to pray through us so that His will might be done.

I recently went through a time when I was involved in a great deal of intercession, and eventually there were days when I didn't want to continue. It was hard work, but during that time I learned that in spite of the reluctance of my own flesh, I could count on the Holy Spirit. Before spending time in prayer I would just say to God, "I'm tired, Father. Please help me," or "Holy Spirit, give me the desire and the energy to keep praying until the Father's will is accomplished. Flow through me; strengthen me."

Later the realization would come that once again the Holy Spirit had strengthened me to pray yet another time with energy and power.

I knew God always enables us to do whatever He asks us to do, but I had never seen it worked out in such a literal way before. The Holy Spirit throughout that time of deep intercession literally became my strength, my encourager, my enabler. He was my faithful companion in prayer.

I was very aware that I would never have been able to get through that kind of intensity in prayer without His help. And throughout the working in prayer that was needed to see His will accomplished, God, through His Holy Spirit, had literally joined me in prayer. I, of course, was very much the weaker vessel in this partnership. But God didn't seem to mind. As long as I was willing, He was faithful to pray through me "with groanings that couldn't be uttered," to invigorate me with His energy, to give me His resolve to keep going when I became discouraged, and to give me His divine rest when I needed it.

Somehow, I want you to become aware of the tremendous gift God has given you because He wants a relationship with you. It is the gift of Himself, in the person of the Holy Spirit. The Holy Spirit is the active part of the Godhead within you. He is truly "God at work" in you.

It is the Holy Spirit who draws us to come to God. It is the Holy Spirit who throws light upon the person of Jesus Christ so that you can see Him and know all He has done in order for you to have a relationship with the heavenly Father. It is the Holy Spirit who opens up the Scriptures so that you can begin to know God's ways. It is the Holy Spirit who continues to work in your life so that God can develop the kind of relationship with you that He had in mind when He first thought of you. It is the Holy Spirit who continues to call you to come to the Father.

It is He who literally comes to live inside you, who stays beside you continually and enables you to fellowship with our heavenly Father. It is His voice you hear when God talks to you. It is His strength you feel when God energizes you. It is His power that will come upon you as you surrender yourself completely to God and ask for the filling of His Spirit.

It is the Holy Spirit who teaches us to pray and to know the Father in prayer. It is the Holy Spirit who brings forth prayer through us that is in keeping with His will and His ways.

And it is the Holy Spirit who takes the relationship one step farther, because in working together in intercession we are finally able to come into a closeness with God that we could gain in no other way.

In intercession, we truly come to know the heart of God as He makes His emotions and desires known to us as we pray. We take on God's heart and His emotions as the Holy Spirit prays His will through us. We begin to feel His emotions of grief over sin, His yearning and desire for a relationship with people, and His overwhelming love for you and me. We begin to know His will, His absolute and unrelenting determination to accomplish His will, and His power to accomplish whatever is needed in given situations.

We begin to see more and more His wisdom, His patience, and His plans for good in our lives and in the lives of others. It is the Holy

Spirit's constant presence and unending help that brings all of this into our lives.

> We do not know what we ought to pray, but the Spirit himself intercedes for us with groans that words can not express.
> —Romans 8:26

> *"Beware of getting ahead of God by your very desire to do His will. We run ahead of Him in a thousand and one activities, becoming so burdened with people and problems that we don't worship God, and we fail to intercede. <u>If a burden and its resulting pressure come upon us while we are not in an attitude of worship, it will only produce a hardness toward God and despair in our own souls.</u>"*
> —Oswald Chambers

Reflect

Have you had "burdens" that weighed you down, causing you to feel disheartened?

Using the statements I use in the text to explain what a prayer assignment (burden) is or is not, think about the "burdens" you may have carried in the past. What kind of attitude did you have at the time? Were they truly prayer assignments?

Study

What does the Lord promise to do in Joel 2:28-29 and Acts 1:8 that will help us with prayer assignments?_____

What does Acts 1:8 say we will receive from the Holy Spirit that will help us to follow through?

_____

Look up Ephesians 6:18. What are we instructed to do always or on all occasions?_____

In chapter 17, we discussed the work of the Holy Spirit with us, in us, and upon us. Do you see the necessity for the "added power" of the Holy Spirit "upon us" as promised in Acts 1:8? _____

What does Romans 8:26-27 tell us the Holy Spirit does? _____

What can fail us? Psalm 73:26 _____

What does Psalm 138:3 say will happen when we cry out to God?

_____

What are we instructed to do in Psalm 55:22? _____

What are we promised? _____

Receiving God's Strength to Pray

Begin to make it a habit to ask the Holy Spirit daily for His help in prayer. He wants to guide and help you.

This week, make yourself available to God for His prayer assignments. Ask the Holy Spirit to enable and empower you to pray according to the concerns of your Heavenly Father. Ask Him to let you feel His compassion and concern for the people or things you are praying for.

Prayer of Response

Dear Holy Spirit,

Pray through me today. I want to pray the will of my Father. Help me to feel His heart for the lost, His compassion for the hurting, and His concern for the world.

Amen.

Something More

And whenever you stand praying, if you have anything against anyone, forgive him, that your Father in heaven may also forgive you your trespasses. But if you do not forgive, neither will your Father in heaven forgive your trespasses.

—Mark 11:25-26

How could this scripture affect a prayer assignment you may have?

To be an effective intercessor, we must get rid of the judgment in our heart toward the people for whom we are praying, or our prayers will be ineffective.

Disapproval and criticism of people's actions must be brought to Christ and exchanged for the loving concern He feels. Our own critical and judgmental spirit (especially when the person for whom we are praying affects us or our loved ones in some way) will pollute and negate our prayers.

Prayerfully consider if this is a problem for you right now in any of your prayer assignments.

Discussion

Share an experience with a prayer assignment you have had in the past.

Ask the Holy Spirit to enable you as a group to pray His prayers for some of the prayer projects you have already started.

CHAPTER 25

Armed and Ready

There is a hill in my neighborhood. It is a big hill; the kind that leaves you gasping for breath every time you trudge up it, no matter how athletic you might be. I don't particularly enjoy climbing it, especially when I am forcing one foot in front of the other and gasping for breath, but I know it is good for me, and I love the "Rocky" feeling I get when I reach the top. You know… arms in the air… pumping up and down.

However! A big dog lives right at the crest of the hill, and whenever I get close to the top, huffing and puffing and just concentrating on putting one foot in front of the other, right before I get to the "Rocky" stage, here comes this dog, snarling and barking and clawing the fence. He completely destroys the elation I would normally feel in nearing the top of the hill.

Oh, there are a few times when I am able to sneak by, but not many; even when he is in the garage, he still seems to know I am out there. I try to be as silent as possible—try not to gasp for breath too noisily—but somehow he always hears me and out he runs to bark, growl, and snap at me until I get past his yard. Some days I just want to yell back at him as loudly as he is barking at me. The solution would be to not walk that way—but I like conquering that hill. There aren't any others as steep that give as good a workout in such a short time… if only there wasn't a dog…

After years of the up and down (mostly down) struggles of owning his own business, Chuck finally sold it to a much larger company and went to work for them, managing a branch office. It should have been a lucrative and rewarding time for us, with less pressure and responsibility, but as Chuck began his new job in a beautiful corner office with wrap-around windows, spectacular views, and expensive executive desk, he soon became aware that the beauty of his surroundings was offset by the destructive behaviors, sad personal problems, and spiritual blindness of the people he worked with. The stories he brought home were amazing, and we became aware of just how "dark" this new environment was. We started to pray for his coworkers, and as I began to meet some of them at social events, the prayer list grew longer and longer. I was acutely aware of the possibility that perhaps no one had ever prayed for some of these people.

One year led to another, with little effect from our prayers. At the same time, the supposedly easy and lucrative job began to involve nothing but problems and headaches for Chuck. I don't remember how long he had been working there when I awoke to yet another day of depression, problems, and minor yet irritating sickness within my household. That day, however, the realization that this wasn't normal finally broke through the just-slog-through-it fog I had been living in. I called a friend and asked her to come and pray with me.

She came over that morning, and we sat down and began by asking the Lord for wisdom and discernment in how to pray. My friend started by asking God to intervene. She prayed over the various situations I had listed, but soon her voice became bolder as she asked for God to deliver us from "spiritual forces of wickedness" (Eph. 6:12). In her prayer, she quoted scriptures about the supremacy of Jesus Christ, our authority in Him, and His victory over all the works of the enemy, as well as other promises from God's Word.

I listened to her pray, and it was like a covering was removed from my eyes as I began to see the circumstances I had been living in under a new light. Until then I hadn't made any connection between the problems we were having and the prayers I had been praying for souls at Chuck's workplace.

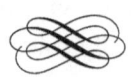

When you have begun to develop a relationship with God which includes earnest intercession, you will begin to walk up some steep hills in prayer. You are going to be flexing spiritual muscles and you will begin to see results from your prayers. While you are conquering those spiritual hills, you are going to be tramping on ground that Satan feels is his territory. Since he knows that intercession is the single greatest threat to his kingdom, you can expect him to try to frighten or distract you; to do whatever he can to keep you off those hills of intercession. Chuck and I, because of our prayers, had begun to walk in an area that Satan felt belonged to him. We had awakened the dog, and he was desperately trying to frighten us off what he felt was his territory.

> *For we do not wrestle against flesh and blood, but against principalities, against powers, against the rulers of the darkness of this age, against spiritual hosts of wickedness in the heavenly places.*
> —Ephesians 6:12

By keeping us concerned over our own problems, Satan felt he could distract us and keep us from praying for others.

Perhaps you would rather not think about Satan or have to deal with him in any direct way, but as you grow in your relationship with God, whether you are an intercessor or not, you will, at some point, be confronted with the need for spiritual warfare. Although the topic of spiritual warfare is sometimes taken too far in Christian circles, bringing confusion and a kind of myopic view of circumstances and Satan's involvement in them, we cannot go to the other extreme and ignore the fact that we have an enemy, and the people for whom we are praying have an enemy as well. *"....your adversary, the devil who walks about like a lion, seeking whom he may devour..."* (1 Peter 5:8). Therefore you and I must be prepared to experience the conflicts that will come into our lives. We need to learn to recognize his tactics and how to effectively stand against him in the power and authority of Jesus Christ.

Learning to Pray

Therefore take up the whole armor of God, that you may be able to resist in the evil day, and having done all, to stand.
—Ephesians 6:13-14 (NASB)

We are told three times in the warfare passage in Ephesians 6:10-18 to stand! This means we are not to give way in any conflict with the enemy of our souls. We must understand that conflict and suffering, because of Satan's role in the world, are a part of life on earth. We need to be prepared to experience the conflicts that will come, knowing God will use it to perfect, confirm, strengthen, and establish you (1 Peter 5:10 NASB).

I don't have time in this short chapter to give you a complete course in spiritual warfare but the most important point to remember is God is always in control and Satan can never operate in a believer's life without His permission. Most of the sickness and problems in our life are the result of living in a fallen world but there are times when there is more direct involvement by the enemy of our souls. This is allowed by God only if it serves His purposes in our lives. Job is a perfect example of that. Satan was allowed to afflict him for a season because it served God's intentions for good.

"We can see from the recorded conversation God had with Satan that God was proud of Job. However, He was also ready to mature him. He wanted to deepen Job's faith, to deal with his pride in his own righteousness and to draw him into a closer relationship. At the same time God was creating a history of the events that would be used to bring wisdom and peace to the hearts of people throughout the ages." Learning to Trust God, Deborah Kern

Even though we can feel like Job at times when things in our life are going terribly awry, few of us will suffer like he did. But as He did with Job, God has a purpose when He allows the enemy to break through a small part of the protective covering surrounding us as children of God. Those purposes are many and varied and are usually related to the need for maturing in some area. It could also be a signal we are on the right tract spiritually, perhaps stepping into new areas of spiritual growth. That kind of step almost always brings some kind of attempt at distraction by the enemy of our souls.

And like Job, it may be allowed because it will enable us to know God and experience God in a new and deeper way. He wants us to learn to run to Him as a child does a loving father when someone is hurting them; He wants us to learn to know and experience Him as our deliverer and protector; and He wants us to learn to know Him as our comforter when we are hurting because of the losses Satan causes. He also wants to draw us into the camaraderie of a working relationship as we stand together with Him against the enemy who attacks us and countless others.

Most of the time the attacks are in our mind; usually thoughts of fear and worry. Thoughts that bring dissension with others are also a much-used tactic and will come in the areas where we are vulnerable because of a lack of maturity. There may be times however, when the warfare is a direct result of the intercession we may be involved in.

Part of learning to pray involves learning to work with Jesus in spiritual warfare. There will be times when the deliverance you need and the answers to prayer you are looking for will depend upon your willingness to resist Satan (1 Peter 5:8), and to faithfully follow the instructions in Ephesians 6:10-18 to put on the full armor of God and do battle with the enemy. This armor is to be worn daily as a way to be clothed and protected from Satan's attacks, and every part of the armor is necessary in our struggle against "spiritual hosts of wickedness" v.12. Often, the struggling will take place defensively in our thoughts and emotions as we wrestle against temptation, depression, fear, turmoil with others, and untruths about the character of God. The armor, more than anything else, is a way to guard ourselves from the lies (darts) thrown at us by the "wicked one."

But there will be days when you will have to engage in more active warfare than just putting on the armor of preparedness. God would never have given us this metaphor if He didn't know we would need it in times of battle with the enemy. Warfare is part of intercession, and when we fail to allow God to direct us in this kind of prayer, we can waste a lot of energy praying over symptoms and problems when the right response is to "resist" the devil (1 Peter 5:9). We raise our shield of faith and use the sword of the Spirit by meditating on and quoting God's words of truth. At times, the most effective prayer you can pray will be to proclaim the truth of Christ's complete victory over the enemy.

Learning to Pray

The following excerpt is from a book on spiritual warfare by Thomas B. White:

> Many people mistakenly think that dealing with the evil one requires some deep level of knowledge and a super-spirituality and that it involves a long, laborious struggle. Jesus identified Satan as the "father of lies," the master of deceit. As such, it is the truth of the Word of God that dispels and expels the lies. While many of the devil's devices may appear complex, breaking them is scripturally simple. <u>Faith</u> in the supremacy and sufficiency of Jesus' name (Matthew 11:22-24; Matthew 18:18-20), <u>confidence</u> in the power of his atoning blood (Revelation 12:11), <u>courage</u> to claim and use our authority in resisting evil (Luke 10:19) and total <u>trust</u> in the imminent power of the Holy Spirit (Acts 10:38) will break oppression. Dealing with evil requires tools the ordinary Christian has at hand. The Lord will move according to his purpose if conditions for victory are being met. Dealing with the deceiver requires a "go for it" kind of spiritual guts that engages the gears of faith.
>
> <u>Pray</u>....reaffirm through praise...repent of any known sin... ask in prayer for God's wisdom (James 1:5,6) and a sharpening of discernment (1 John 2:20,27). Invite the Holy Spirit to take full control of the circumstance you are facing.
>
> <u>Realize your position in Christ</u>. Think of your true identity as enthroned with the Savior (Ephesians 2:6).
>
> <u>Rely on the supremacy and sufficiency of Jesus' name</u> (Philippians 2:9-11), on the power of his atoning blood (Colossians 1:13-20; Revelation 12:11).
>
> <u>Remove the ground of oppression.</u> Moral compromise, deception, and exploitation of vulnerabilities are the chief avenues used to influence people.
>
> (Thomas B. White, The Believer's Guide to Spiritual Warfare (Ann Arbor, Mich: Servant Publications 1990) page 46-50.)

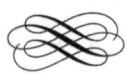

If this subject is new to you I encourage you to learn more about it, using either the book quoted above or Kay Arthur's book *Lord, Is it Warfare*. They will bring invaluable knowledge to you.

Remember, like every kind of praying, spiritual warfare must be kept within the framework of our relationship to God. It is never reactionary in the sense that our response is not to the devil. If we are diligent in asking the Holy Spirit to direct our prayers, *He* will reveal when spiritual warfare is needed. The priority given in James 4:7 is to "*submit yourselves to God*. Resist the devil, and he will flee from you" (emphasis added).

The result will be victory over numerous problems in your life and in the lives of others. As well, your relationship with Jesus will deepen in new ways as you literally begin to experience the battlefield camaraderie that soldiers, who walk into battle together, experience because you are walking into battle behind your Lord and Savior, Jesus Christ, WHO IS ALWAYS VICTORIOUS over the enemy.

When Chuck began working for the new company, he experienced many problems. At the same time, we were under attack in other areas. It seemed odd to me at the time, but eventually I realized that having to wait for victory kept us praying. It kept our hearts stirred up, and as we came back again and again to God to find His will in prayer, we were often stirred to oppose Satan's attacks. When we prayed, we knew we were to pray for the people of the company. God would pour out His compassion for them, and increased energy to keep asking for souls and claiming them for the kingdom of God. Would we have prayed that fervently and that often over those people if we hadn't literally been driven to do so in response to Satan's attack on us personally? Probably not.

As we walk more in intercessory prayer, spiritual warfare will become an absolutely necessary part of our prayer life, but it must always be set against a background of complete trust in God and in His ability to take care of His children. When we are looking to God's

Word for instruction in spiritual warfare, we mustn't forget the countless scriptures on God's faithfulness, His ability to take care of us, and the peace He has for us.

In and through every attack on us personally, God was faithful. He never allowed anything to happen to us unless it could be used for greater good in our lives and in the lives of our children. God never wastes anything. As I look back and think about different times when we were under obvious attack, I see that God also used it for so much good, and our family experienced important growth in many ways, not just in spiritual warfare.

> *The Lord will rescue me from every evil attack and will bring me safely to His heavenly kingdom.*
> —2 Timothy 4:18

> *And the God of all grace, who called you to his eternal glory in Christ, after you have suffered a little while, will himself restore you and make you strong, firm and steadfast."*
> —1 Peter 5:10

Instead of being a cause for fear or anxiety, eventually we will begin to see attacks of Satan for what they are: the desperate barking of a dog behind a fence, trying to protect territory that is not his. That barking should always signal us that God is ready to move. He is ready to bring victory and deliverance in yet another area, and it should bring excitement to our hearts at the same time it is driving us to our knees to pray until God's victory is complete.

Years after Chuck had begun working for the new company, he came home one day and said, "I met a guy named Jay today. He just took a job with us. It seems we met him years ago when we went to dinner in the home of a woman who worked for me at that time. They were both divorced and living together. Do you remember that? He worked for a rival company back then. Well, they broke up and he moved to Seattle, but he recently moved back to work for us. He came in to introduce himself and told me we had met before. He then told me the story of how he became a Christian while in Seattle, married a Christian woman, and now has a son.

I thought for a moment, and then looked at Chuck in amazement. "His name is Jay? I do remember him! That night when we came home from the dinner party, I knew I was to pray for him. It seemed odd at the time, but God directed me to pray for him so specifically, even though the woman was more familiar because you worked with her. I wrote his name in my prayer diary and prayed for him very diligently for awhile, but I haven't thought of him for years. Wow. He's a Christian? I think I still have that diary somewhere with his name in it."

And Jay, who momentarily wandered into my life and then out again during that time of intense intercession and spiritual warfare, was now a part of God's forever family. His heavenly Father, who knows those who will answer the call to salvation, and moves people in and through one another's lives with His eternal purposes in mind, briefly moved Jay into mine. I don't often see the results of prayer when I am praying for people groups in other countries, people in my neighborhood or others God brings across my path to pray for from time to time. This time, however, God was able to encourage me years later, reminding me that the prayers I pray in obedience to His direction, and the small sacrifices I make to do so, have eternity written all over them.

Personal Reflection

Have you ever felt there might be unseen powers manipulating circumstances to bring problems, physical illnesses, and the temptation to sin?

Do you struggle with fear, depression, anger, obsessive thoughts, confusion, or unbelief?

Do you feel there might be "strongholds" of sinful behaviors, addictions, or compulsions in your life that are kept in place by the enemy of your soul?

Learning to Pray

Scripture Study

Look up 1 Peter 5:8-11. What does Peter warn us about? _____

How is Satan described? _____

What are we to do? _____

What is God going to do? _____

What should be the ultimate effects of the suffering we endure because of Satan's attacks on us (verse 10)? _____
_____

What four things are we told to do in James 4:7-8? _____
_____

What warfare principle is given in Deuteronomy 23:9? _____

What did Jesus give the disciples before sending them to proclaim the kingdom of God? (Luke 9:1-2) _____

What promises does Jesus give the disciples in John 14:12-14? _____

What is given to Peter (and us) in Matthew 16:19? _____

What are we promised in 2 Peter 2:9 and 1 Corinthians 10:13?
_____

What principle of spiritual warfare is exemplified in the story told in 2 Chronicles 20:1-30?
_____

    There are numerous principles to be learned about intercession and spiritual warfare—but probably the most important truth is the power of praise and worship in routing the enemy. Praising God in times of problems erects a defense around us (shield of faith) and brings the courage we need to be able to stand firm against the enemy's attack.
    What two things does Psalm 149:6 link together?

Look up 2 Cor. 10:3-5. Think about the types of strongholds that may affect your thinking and prayer life such as unforgiveness, fear, anger, greed, resentment, hatred, guilt, or unbelief. These attitudes can pollute our lives and will make us vulnerable to the enemy's attacks. Consider the weapons God gives us to overcome strongholds: prayer, the Word of God, faith, and the power of the Holy Spirit.

Read Romans 12:1 & 2 and ask God to transform and renew your mind and set you free from any type of stronghold.

Receiving God's Authority to Resist Satan

Begin today to talk with God about the need for spiritual warfare in dealing with some of the circumstances you are facing. Tell Him you are willing to learn about this aspect of prayer.

Discussion

Discuss any experiences you may have had with spiritual warfare.

Discuss the various pieces of armor in Ephesians 6:10-18

CHAPTER 26

Untangling Lives

Wednesday. Laundry day! Not my favorite job at any time, but today it seemed even worse. I was discouraged. Even prayer hadn't helped. I had gotten up off my knees as depressed as I was when I knelt down.

I was feeling such a sense of heaviness, a sense of futility in my praying. I had been praying for many months about a situation we were involved in with our business and, at the same time, for a dear friend who was experiencing difficulties. Even though I had been learning much about intercession, I was becoming weary of it all and beginning to question why it was taking so long to see any answers. I had begun to wonder about the efficacy of prayer. All the seemingly unanswered prayers I had prayed for people over the years had begun to come to my mind, robbing me of my faith and will to continue.

I trudged toward the laundry room thinking that maybe I could get something else done. When I walked by my bedroom I decided, in a burst of spring-cleaning fervor, to wash the large custom-made comforter that covers our bed. I usually have it dry-cleaned, but since I had a new large-capacity washing machine, I decided I could save the $25. So without a lot of thought, I stuffed it all down into the washer, set the machine on its gentle cycle so it wouldn't tear the 12-inch lace trim, added a little detergent, and started it up.

When I came back a half hour later, I opened the lid to find my huge comforter compacted tightly around the agitator in an incredibly small mass. Alarmed, I reached in to pull it out. It was stretched so tight that it was hard to grasp anything, but I gently grabbed some material and gave a little tug. It didn't move. I reached down further into the washer to lift it out from the bottom. I still couldn't catch hold of anything.

Learning to Pray

With rising horror I tried again to pull even a part of it out, but I couldn't pull any part of it away from the agitator. It had become so tightly twisted and pulled around the agitator that it wouldn't move even an inch. The ends were tucked back inside somewhere so I couldn't grasp anything to try to unwind it. I couldn't pull anything away because there was lace trim everywhere, which would rip if I tugged too hard.

I fought down the feeling of panic as I tried to gently pry it loose. I worked and pulled, but every time I got an area worked loose a little, I found it was attached to lace that was jammed tightly into another section. It was fast becoming a nightmare.

After about a half hour of pulling and twisting and trying to maneuver it, I realized I was going to have to get the agitator out and then work on it. I ran to the phone and called Chuck at work to ask how to do it.

"Oh, you just take off the top of the agitator and unscrew a bolt and it should just lift out," he answered breezily.

"Okay," I thought, "I can do this."

I went back to the laundry room and tried to pull the comforter off the top. It was a good idea, but it wasn't going to work: The comforter was wrapped around and over the top of the agitator in such a way that I couldn't get to it.

So I started in again, trying to gently pull just one section free. The part at the bottom of the washer seemed more workable, so I reached down and began to pull and dig through layers of material and lace trying to release an end so I could unwind it from the agitator. I worked and worked until my arms were aching with the effort of it all. Several times the thought came to mind, "Boy, I really needed this today!" Frustration was mounting as I despaired of ever getting it free.

Several times I had to stop and do something else because my arms were so tired, but I kept coming back. Visions of having to cut my comforter off the agitator would fill my mind and give me renewed energy. Finally, as I was struggling, pulling and twisting, pushing and tugging, desperately trying to work another section free, I began to cry. I was just so frustrated with it all, with everything!

"God, please help me," I whispered in desperation.

Suddenly, into the middle of the struggle to free my beautiful comforter from the twisted trap that looked like its ruin, I heard God's voice.

"This is what it is like when I am working to untangle all the separate pieces of the situations you've been praying about for so long. It sometimes takes a great deal of complicated and time-consuming work.

"And this is what it is like when I am working to set someone free from the pain and bondage that a sinful world has forced upon them. Sometimes the lace of their lives has to be handled carefully, requiring endless hours of gentle maneuvering so that it won't be destroyed as I work to bring light and truth into their life."

My hands were instantly stilled as I thought about the feelings of discouragement I had been carrying throughout the last few weeks and the questioning that had been choking off my faith and the will to continue in prayer.

Now, with my hands plunged deep into the washing machine, understanding began to flood the drained and empty desert of my spiritual being. Tears of joy, instead of frustration, began to flow.

As I thanked God for new insight, I was filled with fresh purpose and rejuvenated faith. I began to attack that comforter with renewed energy and at the same time I prayed again for my friend and for the concerns that had seemed so heavy only hours before.

As each new section of my comforter worked free, I also experienced a freeing of my faith and a new certainty that God was working in the life of my friend and in the seemingly impossible situation Chuck and I were personally facing.

When I finally pulled the comforter out, with not one tear in the lace, I hugged it to me.

"Thanks, Father," I whispered as I took comfort in the knowledge that God would continue to work until the complex, time-consuming effort necessary to answer my prayers was finished, "...for everything!"

As we continue in intercession we will be faced to an even greater degree with God's timing in answering our prayers. It can be hard to understand why some things seem to require so much prayer and others so little. The relative importance of the thing being prayed for doesn't always seem to correlate with the amount of prayer. There isn't a clear pattern at all.

And so it's difficult to keep praying when we feel God should have already answered a request. We see only the obvious goal of our particular request, and we see it through the tunneled vision of our own impatience.

We tend to put things in categories, viewing them from the perspective of how difficult the answer to our request seems to us, what answers we've received to previous prayers that were similar, what we've seen and heard regarding answers to prayer in the lives of others, a few applicable Scriptures such as "Ask and it shall be given you"—and it still doesn't make sense!

Maybe you've noticed this.

Answers to prayer take time. Sometimes a lot of time!

It's frustrating to us. We would like to see God's miracle power on an hourly basis. We would like to see our loved ones saved immediately, receive instant help in times of need, be able to call down fire on our enemies, witness countless healing miracles, and see the fulfillment of our every desire.

All those immediate answers would certainly solve a lot of problems for us. We would get things taken care of and have a lot more confidence in God at the same time. It would take the pressure off.

Yes. That's definitely what we need—instant answers!

Most of the time however, that isn't what we get. Answers to prayer seem to take a lot more time and a lot more prayer than we might have thought necessary when we first started to pray over a matter.

As we looked at prayer in terms of relationship, we saw that perseverance in prayer is a way to connect us with God over and over again. Each time we come because a matter is very important to us, we make progress on the path of surrender to His will, cleansing, maturity, and further knowledge of God Himself.

But when we look at the realm of intercession, we begin to see a different reason for persistence in prayer. We live in a universe controlled by the physical laws of nature and by the causes and effects of the actions of sinful people. To ensure free will, God has limited Himself to intervening in the world primarily in response to our request for Him to do so.

To answer our prayers, God must sometimes use an indirect approach, subtly moving and directing events and lives, while not crossing over self-imposed boundaries that ensure man's freedom to choose whether he will have a relationship with God. This sets up many varied situations in which God must work to answer prayer, not the least of which is the need for continued striving with sinful and rebellious people.

At some point you may have noticed that some familiar Old Testament stories seem to paint a picture of a God who must be persuaded to act differently than He desires: Jacob wrestling with the angel of the Lord until he received a blessing; Abraham bargaining with God over Sodom and Gomorrah; Moses interceding for the Israelites when God wanted to destroy them.

Is this another aspect of intercession? Is it continuing to pray over a matter until you change God's mind?

One of the stories mentioned above might help shed some light on this question. After being miraculously delivered from the hand of Pharaoh, led safely across the Red Sea, provided with water from a rock, and supernaturally given manna every day, the Israelites came to Mount Sinai. There they literally heard the voice of God. Never before had God reached out to a group of people that way. But when Moses stay on the mountain grew lengthy, the children of Israel became impatient and built a golden calf to worship.

God was justifiably enraged. He told Moses what was happening down in the camp and said, "Now leave me alone so that my anger may burn against them and that I may destroy them. Then I will make you into a great nation" (Exodus 32:10). Quite a switch from the loving, providing God who had performed miracle after miracle to free them from Egypt and had supernaturally continued to care for them. Their blatant sin in making an idol drove God to anger and a desire for quick and deadly justice.

But Moses began to intercede until "the Lord relented and did not bring on his people the disaster he had threatened" (32:14).

At first glance, this story seems to present a picture of an angry, fed-up God who must be talked out of destroying the Israelites. Is this what intercession is all about? Is this what was happening when Abraham bargained with God for Sodom and Gomorrah?

Not quite.

We must remember that God's character is multifaceted. One part, His righteousness or holiness, demands justice while another part, His love, demands mercy. When man's sin weighs down the balancing scale so far that God's requirement for justice begins to come to the forefront, then intercession will add weight to the side of God's mercy. This enables God to continue to strive with mankind to bring about redemption, repentance, and change.

Allowing man free will and yet intervening in response to prayer takes intricate maneuvering on God's part. His work in the world and in the lives of mankind is much more involved than you and I can see, and during this maneuvering there is often a need for someone to hop up on the balancing scale on the side of mercy and intervene for the unbelieving, for the rebellious, for the spiritually blind or indifferent.

More prayer is also necessary when Satan is determined to resist God's will in any matter (Daniel 10:1-14). As our last chapter pointed out, it is important that we learn to discern when there are unseen forces opposing God's will that require us to persevere in prayer.

Another point evident in this story is that God knows where and when intercession will be needed, and He looks for men and women who will take up the work of interceding so His will can be done.

God knew the Israelites would turn from Him and drive Him to anger, so He placed someone (who had come to know His character enough to confidently appeal to His mercy) into the situation who could stand between Him and the object of His wrath, someone who could stand with God on the side of mercy. This is a beautiful picture of our Lord Jesus who daily intercedes for you and me. It is also an example of the kind of work you and I can be involved in. We, like

Jesus, can become intercessors for the needs of those around us, standing beside God on the side of mercy and patience so He can continue to work in people's lives.

God does not want anyone to perish who would accept Christ, but at times the work involved in bringing a lost soul to the point of receiving Christ as Savior is long and involved. God must work within the limits He has imposed upon Himself to ensure free will. Intercession is needed for millions of people who come to God for salvation and who need the hand of God to bring spiritual maturity and growth.

In Ezekiel 22:30 the prophet, speaking for God, said, "I looked for a man among them who would build up the wall and stand before me in the gap on behalf of the land, so I would not have to destroy it, but I found none."

God needs men and women who will stand in the gap and work with Him. Men and women who will continue asking for His mercy, asking for His divine intervention, so that He can continue to deal with man and so His will can be done!

Reflect

What was the reason Jesus gave for sharing the story about the importunate widow? See Luke 18:1

God doesn't want us to lose heart when answers to prayer seem so long in coming. We have to understand that we never see the whole picture and our perseverance in prayer is an expression of trust in Him, believing He is working in response to our prayers.

Study

What instruction does Isaiah 62:6-7 give those who were praying for Jerusalem?

Learning to Pray

Read Exodus 17:8-15.

Notice that the outcome of the battle depended upon Moses' *continued* appeal. Verse 11 says when "Moses held up his hands." This is a beautiful expression of appeal to God, or intercession.

Think about Moses and Aaron and Hur standing on a hill watching the battle below, seeing the change that came every time Moses raised and lowered his hands. The battle seemed to depend more upon him than the men fighting...

Where does the battle take place when we pray? Ephesians 6:12

_____

When we are praying over a matter, what is God seeing? Job 28:24

_____

What does Ecclesiastes 8:16-17 say about God's work on earth?

_____

What does Romans 11:33 say about God's insights? _____

What does Deuteronomy 29:29 tells us belongs to God?

_____

What does 2 Peter 3:8-9 say about God's time?

_____

Ecclesiastes 3:17? _____

What event in Moses' life followed his intercession for the children of Israel in Exodus 33:12-23? _____

What did Moses ask for? _____

God's answer to our desire to come closer, to see His glory, is always "yes." However, there is a part of God you will never know until you learn to work with Him in intercession: until you bring your heart, your emotions, your time, and energy, and unite with God in praying for His will to be done on earth.

Following through in "working" prayer and prayer assignments brings blessings from God, the most wonderful of which is increased intimacy.

His blessings, rest, and provisions will all come to those who become intercessors. If you would like more time to pray, start taking time for intercession. God will increase the time available to you when He sees you are faithful in prayer. He does this by blessing the other parts of our lives with His grace and help. (That doesn't mean that you'll never have to sacrifice to pray, but when we are faithful, He pours out His help and blessing!)

Receiving God's Call to Intercession

Look up Ezekiel 22:30 and underline it in your Bible. If you are willing to become that man/woman, write the words "I will" next the scripture and put a date by it. Then pray a prayer of commitment to God, asking for His help in carrying it out.

Discussion

Share with the group any answers to prayer you have received that seemed to take a long time.

CHAPTER 27

Reaching for True Faith

> But when he asks, he must believe and not doubt, because he who doubts is like a wave of the sea, blown and tossed by the wind. That man should not think he will receive anything from the Lord; he is a double-minded man, unstable in all he does.
>
> —James 1:6-8

Now I would be willing to bet that the above is not your favorite Scripture. It contains the kind of teaching that makes us squirm a little, since most of us have been in the position of feeling extremely double-minded.

These words can send us into despair when we are desperately seeking something from God and aren't sure if He will answer. At times our faith, or lack of it, so condemns us that we find it nearly impossible to pray or believe God could answer our prayer. We hear sermons and teaching on faith and how necessary it is if we are to receive something from God, but nothing appears to happen. We read scriptures like these and immediately feel condemned. We know we don't have enough faith.

We ask God for things, yet at the same time we are not sure if He will answer or if He will give us what we ask for. For some people, "faith" just becomes a bugaboo word that conjures up faith healers, half-remembered teachings on the need for faith, and huge feelings of inadequacy regarding our own faith.

The problem is that we think of faith as something different than our relationship with God. We think of it as something outside ourselves that we must "put on," or a kind of mental exercise.

Some teaching on faith has left us with a distorted idea about what faith really is. Many people think it is just a matter of not allowing any negative thoughts to come into their mind. Others think it means never saying anything but positive, faith-sounding words. These people go through all sorts of mental and verbal calisthenics to make sure they are thinking and speaking the right things, and they surmise that is faith.

I was talking to a friend about a discussion she had been drawn into at her Bible study. They were discussing a member of their church who was undergoing chemotherapy for ovarian cancer. The prognosis for this type of cancer is not usually good, since it often isn't discovered until it has invaded other organs. But the church had been praying for this young wife and mother, and the women were discussing the latest discouraging report and how to pray. One woman became very upset when someone started a sentence by saying, "If she doesn't get better..." She immediately began to chastise the speaker for saying such a thing. To her way of thinking, positive thoughts and positive talk were the keys to faith and healing.

This is the kind of error we can fall into when we think of faith as something different than our relationship with God. We had enough faith to come to God believing in Him for salvation, but somehow, when it comes to praying and receiving what we ask for, we assume that another kind of faith is required: more faith, better faith than what we already have, something that must be conjured up. We forget one of the basic principles of the Christian life is that God gives us what we need. God provides all we need as we reach out to receive.

In the matter of faith, we hear a great deal about how to build our faith by reading the Word, speaking the Word, rebuking doubt and fear, and so on, and there is value in all these things. But we must never forget that the underlying principle in our Christian life is relationship with God. All that He does and seeks to do in you and me comes back to that.

God is not worried about capitalizing on your doubts or uncertainty, saying, "Aha! I knew you didn't really believe. There's no way I'm going to answer your prayer now!"

The disciples tried to cast a demon out of a boy brought to them while Jesus was on the Mount of Transfiguration, but they could not. When Jesus came and the boy was brought to Him, He talked to the father of the boy and said, "If you can believe, all things are possible to him who believes" (Mark 9:23 NKJV).

At that point the father of the child cried out, "Lord, I believe; help my unbelief!"(Mark 9:24 NKJV).

Now have you ever seen a better example of wavering faith or double-mindedness? This father said two different things in one sentence. You and I have more sense than that. At least we try to keep our faith statements and doubt a little farther apart.

Yet the father was not rebuked by the Lord. His statement was actually a very good description of the state of belief present in all of us: belief mixed with doubt.

Jesus healed the boy, and when the disciples asked why they could not drive out the demons, Jesus answered them, "This kind can come out only by prayer" (Mark 9:29).

This wonderful story reveals two keys of faith. The father's faith was mixed with unbelief, yet Christ healed his son. Even though unbelief was present, the father still had enough faith to come to Jesus. That is always the first step.

We must learn to realize that faith is simply "coming to Jesus." Coming to Him is what He desires at all times. Faith is not a state of mind whereby we are in constant control of our thoughts, never allowing a doubt. Faith is coming to our heavenly Father.

Our problem isn't our faith or lack of it. It is that we don't understand that faith, or the essence of faith, is coming to God. And that is something that we can do. We came to Jesus for salvation—that was our first step of faith—and we can keep coming to God. That is enough faith for an answer to any prayer!

This concerned father didn't have the kind of wavering faith referred to in James. His faith was small and imperfect, but it was enough because he came to Jesus. Anytime we have enough faith to come to God, we have enough faith.

Faith is not a state of mind whereby we are in constant control of our thoughts, never allowing a doubt. Faith is coming to our heavenly Father.

This brings us to the second step revealed in this story. When the disciples asked Jesus why they couldn't help the boy, He said their problem was "unbelief," which could also be translated as "distrust." He went on to tell them that with faith as small as a mustard seed they could move mountains (Matthew 17:20). Then He said, "This kind can come out only by prayer" (Mark 9:29).

The disciples had fully expected to be able to perform this miracle. At a superficial level of faith, they expected something to occur because of the words they said. Jesus was telling them that what was needed was not a prescribed prayer, but a life of prayer and its resultant faith.

Jesus reassured them that tiny faith will do, but it must be rooted in a deep personal trust that expects God to work.

There are times in our life when we need more faith. But that doesn't mean we are double-minded. The Scripture in James that sometimes makes us despair of ever having enough faith refers to our attitude toward God, or our faith as it is manifested toward Him. It means we aren't sure we want to come to Him with our need.

Again, the attitude of the father of the demon-possessed boy reflects the right response. He honestly confessed his unbelief and then asked for help. Jesus very willingly gave it. If you have enough faith to come to Jesus, you have all the faith you need, because Jesus will always give us the faith we require.

Again God is not sitting up in heaven testing your faith, waiting for you to goof up so He can say, "See, I knew he didn't have enough faith."

No. When the tests of our faith come, it means He is waiting to give us more faith. It is obviously time for our faith to grow, and He wants to give us the faith that we need in each situation and in each new problem. It is our faith in God that needs to grow, not our faith in the answer.

The key to receiving this faith is prayer. Not a phrase or a style of prayer, or repeating Scriptures over and over, but rather a life of prayer, a relationship with God based on coming to Him again and again. Faith is not praying 20 times instead of 10 times. It is admitting that our faith is inadequate and that we need God's faith in us, and it is then spending time in God's presence until we are confident of His will and know how to pray in a situation.

Reaching for True Faith

There is never any reason to wallow in unbelief and despair in any situation. Whatever God wants to do for you is secondary to what He wants to do in you. First, He wants to increase your faith and trust in Him, then He will help you to pray His will and to stand in faith until the answer comes.

But again and again we must come to the end of our faith and then reach out for His faith. Our problems with faith are not really failures when they cause us to cry out to God for help like the father in the story.

There is so much more God wants to do in us and through us to change our world. But He must continue to stretch us and our faith so that we can walk in peace and trust in Him even when we have to wait for an answer. Then when difficulties cause our faith to be stretched, it won't snap back to its previous capacity but will remain in the new shape and size.

In Romans, Paul tells us that Abraham's faith was accounted to him for righteousness, but if we go back to Genesis and read Abraham's life story, there is quite a bit of evidence of his lack of faith.

Abraham struggled with doubt. At times he took matters into his own hands. Twice he tried to protect himself by lying. He tried to obtain the child God had promised him on his own, failing to wait on God. But though he obviously struggled with doubt, his faith triumphed.

You and I will never become so devoted, our wills so disciplined, and our minds so enlightened that we will not at times doubt God's goodness or His ability to get us out of a situation or bring good from it. There will be times when we may be greatly troubled. There may be times when we are violently shaken, or times when it seems God has forsaken us. However, our faith—the small faith that brought us to Jesus in the first place—combined with the faith God gives us as we come to Him, will enable us to triumph.

The answers we receive during days of adversity will come because of tested and stretched faith. Tested and stretched until we reach the limits of our faith and fall on our knees and cry, "Lord, I believe; help my unbelief."

Knowing what God will do or wants to do all the time is not faith. Neither is always receiving what you pray for.

Faith is choosing to come to God.

The emotions we feel when faced with adverse circumstances or unanswered prayers do threaten our faith and trust in God. Our minds ask a thousand questions. We can plummet so easily into despair when faced with one more plank on the fence of unanswered prayer, one more circumstance that seems to say God isn't listening or God doesn't care, one more day when things don't change. We wonder if God cares, if He's listening, if He's ever going to deliver us, if He's ever going to make sense of it all, if He's ever going to answer our prayers.

What can we do at times like those? Should we pick up another book on faith, or maybe one on prayer or trusting God in adverse circumstances? Should we steadfastly refuse to think those doubting thoughts? Should we force our minds to think "faith thoughts"? Should we quote Scripture and sing faith songs?

All these can help, and there is a time for each, but ultimately our faith and renewed trust must come from God Himself.

Whenever you come to the end of your rope in any situation, whenever you're questioning His goodness or His willingness to answer your prayers, tell God all about it. Tell Him how you feel.

If you don't know what to believe—tell Him.

If you feel He is mistreating you—tell Him.

If you feel He has forgotten you—tell Him.

If you don't know how to pray—tell Him.

If you feel He is waiting too long to answer and will never change the situation—tell Him.

But don't leave it at that. Throw yourself on Him and ask for help. Ask Him to give you the kind of help you need. He knows what to do and how to help you.

He knows if you need grace to keep on trusting in adversity.

He knows if you need to be examined for changes that will be necessary in you before He can change your situation.

He knows if you need to accept His will first so He can use the situation for your good.

He knows how to help you continue in intercession.

And in every situation, God has faith to give you. He has new faith for you to walk in, reassured that He loves you and that He is working out everything for the best. He has Scriptures for you to stand on. He has new grace to enable you to keep trusting.

But you will receive this faith only through prayer—the kind of prayer where you throw yourself at His feet, helpless in your own faith, but choosing to come to Him anyway.

You will receive it only when you've poured out your feelings of anger, frustration, hurt, and fear, and your thoughts of unbelief and uncertainty, and then stayed long enough to receive His grace and help.

You may not always rise from your place of prayer knowing exactly what God will do, but that isn't what is needed. The key is to pray until your heart is at peace, trusting in God. At this point, you can again pray from a position of faith and trust in God. This is absolutely vital for your spiritual well-being, as well as being a key to answered prayer.

Remember, your struggle with unbelief or lack of faith doesn't bother God. It is what you do with it that is important. When it causes you to come to God, you have enough faith:

> Let us fix our eyes on Jesus, the author and perfecter of our faith.
> —Hebrews 12:2

When you begin to spend time in prayer, your knowledge of God will grow and your faith will increase.

> But you, dear friends, build yourselves up in your most holy faith and pray in the Holy Spirit. Keep yourselves in God's love as you wait for the mercy of our Lord Jesus Christ to bring you to eternal life.
> —Jude 1:20-21

Reflect

"When the Lord wants to lead someone to great faith,
He leaves his prayers unheard.
   —Andrew Murray (With Christ in the School of Prayer)

Is your faith being built right now?

> through adversity?
>> through heartache?
>>> through unanswered prayers?

Faith is our positive response to God—our belief in Him and His goodness. But it has to be coupled with a choice to act upon the belief—accepting Christ, obeying His word, trusting during difficult circumstances, and being persistent in prayer.

Study

What do the following scriptures say that reminds us that faith requires continued growth?

Hebrews 10:36-38 _____

James 1:2-4 _____

1 Timothy 6:11-12 _____

Read Hebrews 4:9-11.

What do you feel was the "rest" Paul was talking about? _____

What has God done in your life to bring about rest? _____

_____

Receiving Faith Through Relationship

In times of adversity and stress, when we cry out to God for answers, deliverance, and help, we are doing what Paul calls fighting the good fight of faith.

When we take the time to come and stay in God's presence until our heart is changed, we will always receive new faith.

A life of faith and trust in God and in His goodness is worth every struggle, every dark night of the soul—every fight of faith.

Prayer of Response

Dear Heavenly Father,

I want to live a life of trust in You. Help me each time I waver in my faith to come to You so I can exchange my viewpoint, my worry, and fear for Your truth—truth about You and who You are.

I want to fight for the faith when fighting is needed. Increase my resolve, my dedication, and my strength for the battle. Jesus, I know that You in me will be all I need.

Amen.

Discussion

Share with your group any test of faith you are facing right now. Pray for one another and commit to praying for each other during the upcoming week.

> Build yourselves up in your most holy faith.
> —Jude 1:20

CHAPTER 28

In His Time and Season

"Do you remember my telling you about Anna Marie?" Marci asked excitedly, as soon as we handed our menus back to the server. We had met for lunch and were catching up on recent events, and it was apparent that Marci had just been waiting to tell me about something. She prompted impatiently, "She's the young woman who worked with me for a few months last year."

"Oh, the one you were witnessing to?" I mumbled as I stuffed a piece of warm bread into my mouth.

"Yes. Well, she called me yesterday. I haven't talked to her in more than a year. We caught up on each other's lives, and then she said, 'By the way, I'm reading that book you gave me.'

"Well, Deb, I mentally rehearsed what books I might have given her. I remembered giving her one on raising adolescents because she has a teenage daughter, but I couldn't remember what the other books were, so I asked, 'What book?'

"'Oh, you know,' she replied, 'the Bible.'"

I started laughing. "Ooohhhh, *that* book."

We laughed together for a minute, but Marci wasn't finished with her story.

"You know, Deb, I haven't even thought of her for more than a year, but after she called I looked back in my prayer diary at the period of time she was working in our office. I remember I was very burdened to pray for her for a while, and my prayer diary reflects that, but then she changed jobs and nothing came of it. I stopped praying for her and just forgot all about it. Now I get a call, and it's obvious from the things she said that God has been working in her life."

Marci smiled and reached for the bread as she finished with a sigh of satisfaction. "I've been thinking about this for the last couple of days, and it has really given me increased faith that our prayers do not go unanswered. I can see that even though the prayers God puts on our hearts to pray for people may not bear fruit right away, He is still working."

Prayer often seems to involve something the writer of Ecclesiastes called "times and seasons": "There is a time for everything, and a season for every activity under heaven" (Ecclesiastes 3:1).

There is a time for prayer and there will be a time for the answer to that prayer. The answer may come quickly, or it may come gradually over a long period of time.

Often, you and I, like Marci, will be burdened to pray over a matter for a while, and then the burden goes away in spite of the fact that the prayer is still unanswered. We often just forget about it. When we do remember to pray again, it may be without the same sense of urgency we had originally.

We sometimes think God just didn't answer the prayer, or we conclude the person for whom we were praying wouldn't respond.

However, when we've prayed earnestly in accordance with the written Word of God and the Spirit of God within us for people and situations, those prayers are never in vain; they will be answered.

As we learn to walk in and out of the seasons of prayer that God wants to bring into our lives, the Holy Spirit again will be our guide. He is faithful to help us to pray as we should. He will burden our hearts for those things that God wants us most to pray about at the very time that prayer is most needed.

God will bring prayer needs to our attention both outwardly, through hearing about situations that require prayer, and inwardly, through the gentle prompting of the Holy Spirit. We need to learn to be responsive to Him and willingly spend time in prayer over those concerns. However, we must learn to leave the timing of His answers up to Him. The work of prayer, the season of prayer, will always come before the other things God wants to do.

In His Time and Season

My father is a carpenter, and I can remember days when he would come home exhausted because he and his co-workers were laying the foundation for a new house. At that time, men had to dig the trenches by hand. They don't do that anymore, but laying the foundation is still the most physically demanding part of constructing a home. It involves working with concrete, and the men have to work quickly before the concrete hardens. It is imperative that the foundation be correctly done, or the whole house will be out of line.

Often when you and I pray, we are literally laying a foundation of prayer that will be the groundwork for God's divine plans. There are no shortcuts for this kind of work, and we must not stop until it is finished.

Sometimes God doesn't answer our prayers for a while because we are working on a lot bigger foundation than we realize. So He holds back the answer and at the same time continues to burden our hearts, creating a strong desire for the answer. This causes us to come again and again to pray over the matter, and it is important to persevere in prayer during these times.

It is only later, as events begin to unfold and we see God's hand working, that we may see the whole picture and the extent of the foundation that God was laying down.

Even though we may not immediately see the answer to our prayer, we can be certain that God is working, moving things around, preparing hearts, orchestrating events, and getting things ready—all in accordance with His sovereign plans and according to His perfect timing.

You and I need to become aware of what Paul Tournier calls the "endless complexity of things," because many of our prayers will involve waiting for an answer. It isn't that God is saying no, or that He can't do what we've asked; it's that it will take a great deal more time than we could possibly foresee. God has to move and shift many things and He also has to continue working in us and in the lives of others to prepare things. Time is a very important element when we pray for people. When we ask God to work in someone's life and draw that person to salvation, the process may take years.

Because God so often works behind the scenes, shifting the landscape of our lives and the lives of others too subtly and slowly to be noticed, we often forget that He is there. There is not always a quick return on our prayers. It's easy to lose sight of the fact that God really is listening to our words, that He does hear us, and that the words we say to Him are valuable!

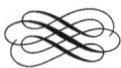

The description of Samuel we looked at earlier, "The Lord was with [Samuel] and let none of his words fall to the ground" (1 Samuel 3:19 NKJV), is a beautiful picture of Samuel's spoken words rising up to the throne of God and God carefully reaching down, taking hold of Samuel's words, and holding onto them so they would not fall.

He does the same with us. We often feel discouraged because we aren't seeing any physical results to our prayers. But we can keep this picture of God reaching down, taking hold of our words to Him, and holding them in His hand while He works unseen in the background until the day we are suddenly struck with the thought, "Oh, this is an answer to prayer. God did not forget what I asked Him."

Sometimes the Holy Spirit has to prompt us, reminding us that we are receiving an answer to a prayer we had forgotten about. I have seen this happen most often in the lives of my children through the years they have been growing up. I've prayed many, many prayers for them: prayers of foundation and pleas for God's hand on their lives, along with countless specific requests. At times I have made a character trait, a talent, or an inclination about which I'm concerned a matter of prayer for a while, asking God to change, to direct, to help. Then, several years later, something happens. I become aware of a change that has been gradually taking place, or an incident reveals that God has been at work in the background, bringing His plans to pass. Suddenly I'll remember the prayers prayed three or four years, or even longer, before.

In His Time and Season

My friend Marci was excited to see the answers to the prayers she had prayed the year before finally bearing fruit in her friend's life. A year, however, isn't really all that long in the spiritual realm. God's activities cannot be relegated to a particular time frame. There are answers to prayers that may not come until many years later.

But even though we don't always see the answers to our prayer, we can be confident that the prayers we prayed in earnest supplication to our heavenly Father have not fallen on deaf ears, but rather have been heard and responded to. They are being held close to His heart until the time He can complete the answer and send it back to us in His time and in His season.

> I am still confident of this: I will see the goodness of the Lord in the land of the living. Wait for the Lord; be strong and take heart and wait for the Lord.
> —Psalm 27:13-14

Reflect

> There is a time for everything,
> And a season for every activity under heaven.
> —Ecclesiastes 3:1

Study

What instruction was given to Habakkuk that we need to remember when God gives us something to pray for? Habakkuk 2:3 _____

_____

What does God promise in Isaiah 42:4? _____

In James 5:7, what does the farmer wait for? _____

What are we instructed to do in James 5:8 and Psalms 62:5?

_____

Learning to Pray

Receiving God's Timing

Look again at Habakkuk. What was Habakkuk told to do in verse 2:2?
_____

Write down your "vision" (the person's name or the desires/concerns you have prayed about, for which you still await an answer).209
_____
_____

Write out a prayer for the person, need, or desire that is your "vision." Ask God to help you to persevere in prayer and also to wait for His timing.
_____
_____
_____
_____
_____

Write the prayer requests you are trusting God to bring about in His time and season in the margin of your Bible next to one of the following verses.

Psalm 52:9

Isaiah 30:18

What can we be sure of as we wait and pray?

Micah 7:7 _____

Discussion

Do you have other scriptures you have claimed as promises for your requests? Share them with the others in your group.

CHAPTER 29

Will You Come?

> Come to me, all you who are weary and burdened, and I will give you rest. Take my yoke upon you and learn from me, for I am gentle and humble in heart, and you will find rest for your souls. For my yoke is easy and my burden is light.
> —Matthew 11:28-30

The purpose of this book has been to remind you that God loves you and desires a relationship with you, a relationship of intimacy and oneness.

Nothing else can bring us the kind of joy, peace, and contentment that an intimate relationship with God can. It will cover every aspect of your life with beauty and purpose, restoration, wholeness, and a sense of destiny.

God's method of establishing that relationship is prayer, and all the types of prayer will connect us to God:

- prayers of tentative overture which begin to establish the relationship as we initially come to God...
- prayers of interaction, questioning, and probing as we begin to deal with God and allow Him access into our lives...
- prayers of desperation when the pain of life threatens to overwhelm us...
- mundane, everyday prayers about the minor, seemingly unimportant things as we invite God to participate in the everyday aspects of our life...
- prayers of communion as we begin to walk with Him in intimacy and daily relationship, learning to know Him in ever greater measure...

- prayers of intercession as we take on His concerns for a lost and dying world and begin to work with Him in making a difference.

Much of our initial prayer life revolves around our neediness; we come because we need help. Since God ordained prayer as the way we receive His assistance, it is never wrong to come to God with our problems and desires. That is what He wants us to do.

However, when we come, while we are in His presence, there is an opportunity for our knowledge of Him to develop. Gradually, as we begin to include Him in the whole of our life, the opportunities for insight into His character and ways begin to escalate.

Our relationship with Him deepens, and we begin to open ourselves more fully to Him. Slowly, the relationship grows more intimate and the center of our existence begins to shift. He becomes the focus of our hearts, and when we come to Him we are not looking as much for help as for the opportunity to be with Him.

If we have allowed the circumstances of our lives to draw us to God, if we are willing to deal with Him in relational prayer, and if we seek Him out in times of sorrow, discouragement, and need, then at some point the grace and help He gives during those times will become secondary to the joy and fulfillment we sense when we are in His presence. We will begin to desire God, not for His help, not for His saving grace, not for His delivering power, and not even for His peace and comfort, but simply for Himself.

God's presence becomes the fulfillment of what we were created to enjoy, giving us a sense of security and love, of belonging, of homecoming.

Please remember that you cannot develop this kind of intimate relationship with God on your own, and in your own strength. No one can, but God provided help for us in the person of the Holy Spirit. It is absolutely essential that you begin to ask Him for help. The best advice I can give you about prayer is that you learn to ask God to help you with it. Daily, continually, ask for help.

"Father, draw me to prayer."

Will You Come?

"Father, forgive me for my reluctance to pray and help me to come to You."

"Holy Spirit, teach me to pray."

"Holy Spirit, help me to pray the will of my Father."

"Enable me to pray Your will."

Every day, these kinds of prayers are giving over our will to the control of the Holy Spirit, and submitting to God's Spirit is always the key to victory. He is very able to do the rest.

A.W. Tozer wisely said, "With the goodness of God to desire our highest welfare, the wisdom of God to plan it, and the power of God to achieve it, what do we lack?" The Holy Spirit was given to us to accomplish all the good in and through us that God has desired and planned.

God is calling you. "Come to me" is His call to prayer, to intimacy, and to fellowship, and His call requires a response from you.

His desire is that you would come to Him and learn to spend time with Him. He wants to develop a relationship with you that is more intimate, exciting, and real than you have experienced before. He wants you to know Him intimately and He desires greater access into your life.

The decision is yours. Will you come closer in relationship? Will you begin to ask for the Holy Spirit's help, relying on Him to enable you to overcome your lethargy and your reluctance?

All of God's intent toward you and toward the world is wrapped up in His desire for intimacy, for relationship, with mankind. When we begin to grasp His purpose, prayer will become not a duty but a means of establishing and deepening our relationship with God, a way to work with Him, a way to know Him, a way to be with Him.

God is calling you to come, to sit at His feet, and to learn to pray. Will you come?

> My heart has heard you say, "Come and talk with me, O my people."
> And my heart responds, "Lord, I am coming."
> —Psalm 27:8 TLB

Reflect

> *Deep within us all there is an amazing inner sanctuary of the soul, a Holy Place, a Divine Center, a speaking Voice, to which we may continuously return. Eternity is at our hearts, pressing upon our time-torn lives, warming us with intimations of an astounding destiny, calling us home unto Itself.*
> —Thomas Kelly (A Testament of Devotion)

I trust there has been a call from God in your life as you have read this book. A call to prayer, a call to know Him in ever deepening relationship, a call to faith and trust, repentance and growth, a call to intercession and perseverance and a call to experience Him more fully. I encourage you to once again answer His call and to commit yourself to prayer.

Study

What does Isaiah 55:6 tell us to do? _____
_____

Read again Song of Solomon 1:4, and underline the first line in your Bible if you have not already done so.

Read also Psalm 27:8. If the words are a reflection of your desire, underline the verse and put the words "I will" next to it, along with today's date.

Receiving God's Call

Remember to ask for and expect God's help in your journey to greater intimacy. An intimate love relationship with you was God's intent before you were even born and He has orchestrated your circumstances toward that goal. He will continue to do so as you respond to His call and allow Him access into your life.

Prayer of Response

Write out a personal prayer of response and commitment below, or in your journal.

Discussion

Discuss the chapters/truths that most ministered to you during your time of reading and studying this book.

Pray for one another, asking for God's help in one another's lives to become seekers of God.

www.ingramcontent.com/pod-product-compliance
Lightning Source LLC
LaVergne TN
LVHW011911080426
835508LV00007BA/341